Historiography

MANCHEStER
1824

Manchester University Press

Historiography
An introduction

Roger Spalding and Christopher Parker

Manchester University Press
Manchester and New York
distributed exclusively in the USA by Palgrave

Published by Manchester University Press
Oxford Road, Manchester M13 9NR, UK
and Room 400, 175 Fifth Avenue, New York, NY 10010, USA
www.manchesteruniversitypress.co.uk

Distributed in the United States exclusively by
Palgrave Macmillan, 175 Fifth Avenue,
New York, NY 10010, USA

Distributed in Canada exclusively by
UBC Press, University of British Columbia, 2029 West Mall,
Vancouver, BC, Canada V6T 1Z2

British Library Cataloguing-in-Publication Data is available

Library of Congress Cataloging-in-Publication Data is available

ISBN 978 0 7190 7285 7 paperback

First published 2007

First reprinted 2009

Printed in Great Britain
by CPI Antony Rowe, Chippenham

Contents

Acknowledgements

We would like to thank Roger Richardson for his support and advice, everybody at Manchester University Press for their encouragement and guidance and Julia Hedley for her assistance in preparing portions of the text.

1

Introduction:
history and historiography

The purpose of this book is to facilitate the critical reading of works of history. We use the term 'history' in at least two ways. It is the word often used to mean the past; and it also means that which is written about the past – historiography or a description of the past. Not all descriptions of the past have to be presented in the form of the printed word, but whatever the medium, the point is that there is a distinction between the past and a description of it. This simple observation, however, is accompanied by a warning that the relationship between those two meanings is a difficult one. We said 'at least two ways' and the variety of value-laden other uses of the term 'history' should also send out warning signals. For example, people talk about something being a matter of historical record, suggesting an incontrovertible record of fact. Similarly, people accuse others of trying to 're-write history', something historians do all the time, an accusation suggesting that there was a perfect match between the actual historical event and previous descriptions of it. Also we are often told that 'history will show' or will judge, vindicating who or what was right and condemning what was wrong, which suggests both accuracy and objective judgement over the long term, when all the information is in and had been assessed, particularly, it is implied, in relation to a self-explanatory course of subsequent history; a popular phrase is 'the verdict of history'. Trotsky was much given to talking about the judgement of history, and Roy Medvedev's critique of Stalinism was called *Let History Judge*. This also suggests that historical events or human actions are assessed in the light of long-term consequences, implying further that the historical narrative is a matter of causal relationships. The judgement may be exercised in terms of whether or not the actors correctly understood the supposed course of history or in terms of a moral judgement upon their motivation or the consequences of their actions; sometimes, and revealingly, no clear-cut distinction is made between the two.

However, another popular term is 'historic', designating something that is worthy of record, which suggests not only that some events or actions are more important than others, but that a principle of selection has to be applied. Should the terms 'historic' and 'historical' be used interchangeably? Perhaps an event considered historic for one generation might not retain its historical significance for later generations. Future generations may discern new significance in hitherto neglected matters, and then have to devise ways of rescuing them from obscurity. Depressingly for historians, the term 'history' can also be used to consign events or people to irrelevance, to a dead past, as in 'you're history' or 'that is now a matter of only historical significance'. This suggests that we should move on from contemplating a dead past that no longer influences us, or at least free ourselves from the past. In contrast to things being of 'historic' significance they now become mere history. These casual usages can often be matched to quite sophisticated philosophies of history and, most importantly for our present concerns, actual schools of historical practice. For example, the philosopher Michael Oakeshott thought that historians had legitimately created a form of historical experience that dealt with 'a dead past' which was 'unlike the present' and was 'the past for its own sake' without practical application.[1] In contrast, what is often dubbed the Whig school of history, which preceded what Oakeshott thought of as a more truly historical school, wrote about history as a story of continuous development which explained the present.[2] This progressive view of history has been described as having 'an exaggerated sense of continuity', resulting in a 'presentist' perspective, meaning that the purpose of the past was seen to be its contribution to the present rather than its having an autonomous existence of its own.[3]

So we should not approach the study of historiography by assuming that our task is a simple one of separating wheat from chaff or, in the case of individual historians, sheep from goats, by checking who best matched their description of the past with the past itself. We could hold to that as an ideal objective, but its attainment is fraught with difficulties; and is an impossible, indeed a meaningless task according to a very vociferous and influential group of postmodernists.[4] In one sense, we have only historiography, not the past itself, because the past, by definition, has gone. Most practising historians will immediately respond to that by saying that we still have, in the present, historical evidence, unmediated records, be they writing on paper or parchment, records of laws, wills or court proceedings, or artefacts dug up by archaeologists, field systems evident still in the landscape, or whatever. This is true, but they do not speak to us directly; they must be interpreted. Alone they are not history in either sense of the term: they are not the past itself either in the sense of a set of empirical facts that speak for themselves or in the romantic sense of the past speaking direct to our historical imagination. History in the historiographical sense is made by us, not by people in the past nor by the record of their actions. Contrary to another popular usage, history does not speak to us directly, even if the source is oral testimony.

We need, therefore, to study the historians who make history. But we cannot study individuals in isolation. There are ways of approaching the past, sometimes self-defining schools of historiography which themselves have a history, and we need to be aware of this. However, we need not be resigned to helpless relativism, merely locating an historian in a particular mind-set or a work of historiography in a particular period or country, and leaving it at that. Nor should we choose an interpretation according to our own prejudices or as a matter of taste – which story we like best. Some historians are more conscientious researchers than others, more accurate, more learned and clearer in their arguments. Many deliberately set out to participate in a continuing debate, perhaps to support an ally or a mentor, or to challenge an opponent. There are established rivalries, even hostilities. Some, one suspects, are being deliberately provocative, perhaps to establish a reputation.

Others have career-defining projects. Some are methodologically explicit; others leave the readers to their own devices. It helps to know about these things. Very few disputes are settled by outright victory, though occasionally a fatal flaw is revealed in the methods, the concepts or the research finding of an influential work. Most arguments peter out because the terms of reference change or because the audience, including review editors and publishers, have lost interest. The study of history has an apparently inexhaustible capacity for moving on and developing new areas of interest, not necessarily because of the discovery of new evidence but because historiography is a product of contemporary society, which is in constant flux. A classic case is the development of women's history; the evidence was often there, but historians had to choose to see it. The past itself cannot demand to be heard; the choice is ours. Methodological failures can occur, and methodological fashions change. For example, under the influence of rampant social science, historians went through a phase in the middle years of the twentieth century of looking for 'models' – of revolution, of dictatorships and so on[5] – and of developing counter-factual propositions using supposedly sophisticated statistical techniques made possible by the use of early computers.[6] In a sceptical postmodern climate these are no longer fashionable.

We cannot ignore some of the philosophical, as well as the general historiographical issues raised by these points, but historians are down-to-earth people and we tend to like concrete instances rather than general theory, so we will endeavour to work mainly through examples. In Chapter 2 we look at the historical profession, its predilections and traditions; the Whig interpretation of history has been chosen to illustrate the relationship between historiography and a prevalent culture because of its central role in the period when the historical profession began to establish itself in England and because of its continuing popular and political influence. Additionally, the critique that demolished the Whig influence in academic circles is illustrative of the supposedly professional 'objectivity' that displaced it and which was subsequently challenged by more relativist approaches. That chapter concludes with an appreciation of the most recent debates between so-called traditionalist and various postmodern positions.

Having established the context in which historical scholarship has to be assessed, we move, in Chapter 3, to a guide to reading historiographical texts, looking at the relationship between 'facts' and 'theories', and at 'meta-narrative' and causation. Examples will include the empiricist–Marxist debate on the French Revolution, class and English social history, and imperialism in the context of globalisation. Students have to read – and then write. So in Chapter 4, we offer a guide to the writing of academic history at undergraduate level, to the skills involved, and contrast this with the non-academic uses of history. Chapters 5, 6 and 7 take three key historiographical topics, important in themselves but illustrative of the issues raised elsewhere in the book. Two are thematic, 'Gender and history' and 'Cultural history', because they represent a broadening of the original, largely political and then economic, interests of early historiography. One, 'The Nazis and historiography', takes a look at the unique fascination that this topic, along with the allied study of the Holocaust, has exercised on both academic and popular historiography. Finally in Chapter 8 we will summarise the main lines of developments in British historiography, the relationships between those developments and academic practice, and conclude with a case for the continuing importance of history. Every chapter includes a guide to further reading.

Notes

1 M. Oakeshott, *Experience and Its Modes* (Cambridge University Press, 1966), pp. 106–11.

2 The monumental classic of the Whig school was W. Stubbs, *The Constitutional History of England in its Origin and Development* (Clarendon Press, 1873) in three volumes. For a brief idea of Stubbs's approach see 'Preface' and 'A sketch of the constitutional history of the English nation down to the reign of Edward I', in W. Stubbs, *Select Charters and Other Illustrations of English Constitutional History from the Earliest Times to the Reign of Edward the First* (Clarendon Press, 8th edn, 1895), pp. v–vi, 1–51.

3 P.B.M. Blaas, *Continuity and Anachronism: Parliamentary and Constitutional Development in Whig Historiography and in the Anti-Whig Reaction between 1890 and 1930* (Nijhoff, 1978), pp. 23–6.

4 The work of Keith Jenkins can reasonably be described as an extreme case of

the postmodern approach. For example, see K. Jenkins, *Why History?* (Routledge, 1999).

5   For the influence of social theory see P. Burke, *History and Social Theory* (Polity Press, 1992); for models in particular see pp. 28–33. For a contrary position, in relation to the French Revolution, see A. Cobban, *The Social Interpretation of the French Revolution* (Cambridge University Press, 1964), pp. 8–14.

6   The most famous or, for some, notorious example was R.W. Fogel and S.L. Engerman, *Time on the Cross* (Norton, 1995), originally published in 1974. For brief introductions to the subject in general and to Fogel's role, see M. Bentley (ed.), *Companion to Historiography* (Routledge, 1997), pp. 483–7; R.J. Evans, *In Defence of History* (Granta Books, 1997), pp. 37–44.

2

Academic history

Introduction

In the 1990s and early in the twenty-first century two apparently contradictory things happened to history. The number of students studying history in schools went down (though not the numbers studying it in universities), while in every other respect history was booming. History on the television, popular biographies and, perhaps above all, family history all reached unprecedented levels of interest. A number of theories have been put forward to account for these phenomena. Family history, for example, has been seen as a way of trying to connect with the past, to find roots, in an increasingly rootless and individualist world. It differs from the other forms of interest in the past because it requires historical research, not passive acceptance, on the part of the interested party. Researchers into family history, not 'professional' historians, dominate the use of county archives. Much information of use to family historians is available online; censuses from 1841 to 1901, for example, and copies of wills up to 1858. The trend away from history in secondary schools and sixth-form colleges may not indicate anything wrong with the way more formal historical study connects with a wider audience; the explanation may lie outside the world of historiography and be more to do with the pressures on the curriculum, including official pressure to have vocational courses and the popularity of certain new subjects. However, although at the time of writing the downward trend in numbers seems to have stopped and was never evident in the universities, it does raise the question of what exactly 'academic' history is and how well it relates to the needs and interests of society.

The rise of academic history

Academic history as we know it – in the sense of being based in academic institutions such as universities, being largely written by academics for students and, one has to admit, for each other – is a fairly recent phenomenon. Before the nineteenth century history was not taught as a separate subject for undergraduates. Classics dominated the curriculum, so the only history that might have been read in pursuit of a degree would have been that of ancient Greece or Rome. A handful of famous historians working outside the universities had produced works for a non-academic audience which are remembered even today. Probably the most famous is Gibbon's *Decline and Fall of the Roman Empire*, still occasionally asked for along with 'the Bible and Shakespeare', to accompany people with their 'desert island discs' as if this classic expression of the ideas of the eighteenth-century 'Enlightenment' was still the ultimate history of the most important event in western history.It would be tempting to suggest that, once history became 'academic', with those overtones of scholarship, professionalism and, thus, objectivity, historiography would retain its value as historical interpretation as well as its literary merit, but there are no last words in historical interpretation. Far from it. Cynics might even say that academic history lost its literary credentials without acquiring scientific ones, but that too would be untrue, for some considerable stylists have written within the academy.

The trend towards academic history is generally thought to have begun in German universities, and its most famous figure was Leopold von Ranke (1795–1886).[1] Ranke did not invent the practice of going to the archives, but he became the best known and most influential of a new breed of academically-based historians, in Ranke's case at the University of Berlin, who wanted to establish history as a prestigious academic discipline. Only through thorough research, argued Ranke, could historians arrive at a true understanding of the past, and it was crucial to his method that the sources be examined critically – to uncover, for example, the motives of the author of a document, as well as its status and veracity. Ideally, he wanted works of history to be objective – he often used 'scientific' terminology in this respect – to be written so as to be true to the past rather than to explain the present, and to be specific to the object under investigation rather than part of some overarching theory about the course of history. This approach is sometimes known as 'historicism' or 'historism', terms discussed in more detail in Chapter 3. He saw history as an antidote to philosophies of history. But, and this is a major qualification, like many of his contemporaries, including the German philosopher, Hegel, he thought in terms of the state as the key component of modern history, and the Prussian state was clearly his ideal state, and the balance of power of the great European states after the defeat of Napoleon was his ideal international state system: he was of course a child of his times as well as a pioneering 'scientific' historian. This coloured his supposedly objective history.[2] The British historian, G.P. Gooch, however, thought of Ranke, 'the master of us all', as objective and motivated entirely by a sense of professional duty rather than political considerations.[3] And, in general, Ranke's reputation abroad was that of the scientific scholar; this led to a misrepresentation of him as fact-minded and non-theoretical, particularly in the United States.[4] It became quite common to think of Ranke as a Positivist.

It is necessary to examine this term, 'Positivist' in the context of the development of modern historiography, for it has been the subject of much misunderstanding. The French thinker, Auguste Comte, can be credited with the development of the term, though several other nineteenth-century figures had similar attitudes and also employed the concept. Comte believed that the only true knowledge was scientific knowledge, and that scientific knowledge could be defined as that which could be induced from observation and, where possible, experiment. With enough observable examples, general laws could be induced. He believed that this was how the natural sciences already operated and that it would be possible for the human or social sciences to follow suit.[5] Comte has a claim, therefore, to be the founder of social science. If history was to become a proper branch of knowledge it had, therefore, to become an inductive science. The observational side of positivism was embraced by what we call empiricism. The empirical method utilises our sensory perception to acquire knowledge, as opposed to introspection or reasoning from first principles, or even faith. It is usually thought of as a very commonsense method, and historians like to think of their Rankean search for evidence as empirical. However, there has been an unfortunate tendency to conflate the terms empiricism and Positivism which ignores the role of inductive reasoning and law-making in the latter. In France there was a patriotic pride in Comte, which led French historians to think of themselves as followers of both Ranke and Comte[6] which was not an association either men would have approved of, for Ranke believed in the individuality of the historical event, avoided generalisation and never set out to establish general laws.[7] In Britain, however, historians, particularly those who were establishing history as an academic subject, were generally hostile to Positivism. They felt that any attempt to establish regularities of human behaviour, to argue that certain conditions might determine human action, challenged the notion of free will and was virtually sacrilegious, at a time when the academic establishment was Anglican, and it was presumed that history showed God's laws, not man's, in operation.[8] This was to become a classic historian's response to any attempt to see patterns of behaviour or to see any organising principles behind human development. It had its origins in nineteenth-century religion, but became adopted as a feature of professional history.[9]

In some ways, however, British historians acquired professional characteristics slowly and reluctantly. It was not until the end of the nineteenth century that one can really talk about professional attitudes in England. Two things had combined to delay professionalisation. Firstly, there was the Oxbridge tradition of educating gentlemen to equip them for their role in society; and then there was the marginally more ambitious desire to educate gentlemanly high-fliers, in particular future political leaders, for whom history was thought to be especially useful.[10] However, by the beginning of the twentieth century, history had acquired a number of university posts, not only at Oxford and Cambridge

but at new universities, like Manchester, and even at the Scottish
universities which had eventually embraced new subjects like history. They were now teaching a number of undergraduates, though
there were as yet no postgraduate schools of history in Britain; you
had to go to Germany for real training as a historian. The first of
the professional journals, the *English Historical Review*, had been
established to publish, without financial reward, articles by pro-
fessionals. The Royal Historical Society provided a professional
organisation, and the Historical Association, with its own journal,
History, and the Institute of Historical Research were shortly to be
established.[11] The British system was never as rigid as elsewhere, as
in Germany for example; in Britain the Ph.D. was never regarded
as an essential professional qualification, and movement in and out
of university careers has remained fairly fluid. Nevertheless, it was
reasonable, by the beginning of the twentieth century, to talk about
a historical profession with its own codes and culture. The process
had begun half a century earlier in the 1850s and 1860s, and it
had been attended by the growth within the academic establishment, particularly at Oxford, of what we might call the first school,
or paradigm, of professional historiography in Britain – the Whig
school of history – and it is to this that we now turn as an example
of a school of history and how it needs to be seen in the wider
cultural context.

The 'Whig' school of history

Historians of the nineteenth century usually think of the term
'Whig' as applying to the moderate reform party that supported
the reform of parliament in 1832, but the term has also been applied to a group of Victorian historians. The Whig historians were
most at home when they wrote about their own English history,
which seemed to them to be the perfect example of the principle of
historical development in operation. They may have been the first
group of historians with academic credentials to write the history
of England, but they were not, of course, the first historians of
England. In fact the very first Englishman, if that is not too anachronistic a term for him, to write the history of the English was the
Northumbrian monk, Bede in the early eighth century. His

Ecclesiastical History of the English People, completed in 731, emphasised 'the progression from diversity to unity' of the English people. This progression was achieved by holy missionaries, the conversion of heroic kings, and was accompanied by frequent miracles, with the English serving God's purpose.[12]

Over one thousand years later the Victorian Whig historians did not deal in miracles, though there was a major debate about this in the increasingly secularised and rationalist intellectual world of the nineteenth century. But they did deal with God's providence and with the special role of the English people. Nor were they entirely immune from the habit of using history to provide examples of wickedness to be avoided and heroic or saintly behaviour to emulate. However, both the Rankean and Comtist schools were opposed to such a use of history, regarding it as anachronistic and unhistorical in the former case, and as primitive, unscientific and unsuitably theological in the latter.

Not all the Whig historians worked in an academic environment; in fact one of the most famous, Thomas Babington Macaulay (1800–59) was more of a literary and political figure – Whig of course. It was Macaulay who did most to turn an explicitly party-political tradition of historiography, which dated back to the earliest interpretations of the English Civil War, into a more generalised national perspective. His *History of England*, which took the Glorious Revolution in 1688 as its centrepiece, was a massive bestseller and a tribute to the continuity of English constitutional government, a key theme of the Whigs, for the Glorious Revolution was a 'preserving revolution' not a destructive one, which would preserve England from further discontinuity, unlike the poor benighted continentals.[13] But the academic establishment disapproved of Macaulay, despite many of them sharing his Whig view of history, and the most influential Whig was probably William Stubbs, not because the sales of his *Constitutional History of England* or his *Select Charters and Other Illustrations of English Constitutional History* could match Macaulay's, but because they became set texts for undergraduates, not only at Oxford, where Stubbs was Regius Professor of Modern History (1866–84), but at Cambridge, and every new foundation, and even every reformed Scottish university, till by the early twentieth century it was impossible to study history in Britain without an acquaintance with Stubbs.[14] Ironically, this most influential 'Whig' historian was a Tory in party-political terms.

He was the most impressive scholar in a trio of friends, who Gooch dubbed 'the Oxford school',[15] the other two being Edward Freeman and J.R. Green. They were all Oxford graduates; Freeman succeeded Stubbs as Regius Professor of Modern History in 1884; and both Green and Freeman assisted Stubbs as examiners. Stubbs's career, however, does illustrate the partial nature of professionalisation in England. He was an ordained Anglican clergyman and his tenure of his Oxford chair punctuated his clerical career, first as an Essex parson and then as a bishop. He never really succeeded in establishing a research school of history at Oxford, in that sense failing to emulate Ranke in Germany. His very appointment, being notionally a royal one and in practice a government one, was due to the fact there was in 1866 a brief interlude of Tory government between the years of Whig-Liberal dominance in the 1860s and early 1870s. He had not yet conducted the research which was to establish his authority and really justify his appointment. The appointment of his successor, the Liberal E.A Freeman, was equally political, Gladstone being in office at the time, and Freeman was too near the end of his career and in poor health at the end of his life to be of much use in developing a new type of research-oriented school of history. Moreover, although he knew the ancient chronicles, he was not a researcher into original documents. In England, professionalisation continued to have its limits.

However, in an age where so much historiography was dedicated to defining the nations of Europe, Stubbs was to play a key role as far as the English were concerned,[16] and he gave his nation a long-lasting Whiggish hue. The Whig historians emphasised – their later critics were to say they over-emphasised – history as a story, a continuity, a development and, by implication, a progress towards a free liberal, enlightened present. The seeds of the present were in the past. For the true Whig historian like Stubbs, no subject illustrated this better than the history of the English nation, especially that unique phenomenon, the English constitution. For

Stubbs, the constitution was not a mere mechanism for protecting English liberties, but the natural product of a national capacity for freedom. As an Anglican clergyman, he was happy enough to incorporate Bede's version of the role of the Church in establishing the initial idea of English unity,[17] but he saw his main task as establishing the continuity of constitutional development from the earliest times. So there were a number of apparent discontinuities that had to be explained away: the Anglo-Saxon invasions themselves were a discontinuity in British history overall; then there were the Danish and Norman invasions; the rule of kings who had more interest in their continental possessions than in England and were hardly to be regarded as purely English at all; the long periods of royal despotism; the dynastic struggles of, for example, the Wars of the Roses. How could all these features of medieval history be explained as part of a continual progress towards the Victorian parliamentary constitution that Stubbs and many of his contemporaries thought the envy of the world? Macaulay had shown how the troubles of the seventeenth century could be incorporated into the Whig story: the Glorious Revolution of 1688, the culmination of the struggle between Crown and Parliament had been a 'preserving' revolution, not a discontinuity. We should note that the Parliamentarians in the build-up to the Civil War earlier in the seventeenth century had claimed, even at the time, to be preserving the rights of the old constitution. The French Revolution of 1789 and the European revolutions of 1848 increased the Victorians' concern to show that destructive revolution was not the English way. The industrial and commercial success of Britain in the Industrial Revolution, and the naval and imperial successes of the period convinced them that the nation was something special and that its history contained the clues to its providential role.

Stubbs had no trouble with the Anglo-Saxon invasion as a discontinuity, for his history was of 'England' which could only begin with the English, so, unlike Bede, he did not start with Britain and the Britons, but with the English in Germany and their tribal assemblies.[18] He established his Whig credentials at once on the first page of his Preface to the Constitutional History: the history of institutions, he said, presents, in every branch, a regularly developed series of causes and consequences, and abounds in examples of that continuity of life, the realisation of which is necessary to give the reader a personal hold on the past and a right judgment of the present. For the roots of the present lie deep in the past, and nothing in the past is dead to the man who would learn how the present comes to be what it is.[19]

And constitutional history was the key branch of institutional history, explained as follows: 'The growth of the English Constitution, which is the subject of this book, is the resultant of three forces, whose reciprocal influences are constant, subtle and intricate. These are the national character, the external history, and the institutions of the people.' Analysis of how these factors operated was impossible, but 'the national character has been formed by the national history' quite as certainly as vice versa.[20] From the sketchiest of sources he inferred a lot about the uniquely Anglo-Saxon freedoms that were brought to Britain. Monarchy, which latterly has become associated with nationalism and patriotism, was something of a problem for Stubbs and the Whigs, because it seemed alien to the concept of self-governing institutions. Stubbs explained it as the product of an 'external' factor: invading war-bands needed war leaders.[21] Later discontinuities were explained away in racial terms: Danes and Norsemen were fellow Teutons with similar institutions, who could be readily absorbed by the Anglo-Saxon majority.[22] Racialism was the ugly side of many of these supposedly liberal Whig historians. Freeman, Stubbs's friend and successor, was the worst offender for he not only saw the positive side of the Germanic races but castigated the supposed weaknesses of others, establishing a hierarchy of races.[23] The Norman Conquest was more problematic for Stubbs because these one-time Norsemen did establish a royal despotism and an oppressive feudal system; and neither they, nor their Angevin successors, could be regarded as purely national leaders. Subsequently, brutal dynastic rivalry seemed to offer little scope for telling a story of progress and constitutionalism. Stubbs's version of events is subtle and well researched but undeniably partisan. It involved a teleological approach; that is, he wrote as if there was an end or purpose towards which everything was struggling. The nation and its institutional embodiment, the constitution, was personified and realised, perhaps dimly at first, but with increasing clarity, its own destiny. Thus, with reference to the thirteenth century:

> The great characteristic of the English constitutional system … is the continuous development of representative institutions from the first elementary stage, in which they are employed for local purposes and in the simplest form, to that in which the national parliament appears as the concentration of all local and provincial machinery, the depository of the collective powers of the three states of the realm.[24]

With Magna Carta, 'The nation becomes one and realises its oneness; this realisation is necessary before the growth can begin … It finds its first distinct expression in Magna Carta'.[25] With Simon de Montfort, 'The idea of representative government had … ripened under his hand; and although the germ of the growth lay in the primitive institutions of the land, Simon has the merit of having been one of the first to see the uses and the glories to which it would ultimately grow.'[26] Edward I was as near as a Whig medievalist could come to having a royal hero because, as Stubbs put it: 'His chief political design, the design of uniting Britain under one Crown, premature as it was at the moment, the events of later ages have fully justified.'[27] Not quite the same version of events as Mel Gibson's blockbuster film, *Braveheart*, but, for Stubbs, this British role was part of the English destiny – just as, for Bede, it had been part of the Church's destiny.

After the thirteenth century, it might seem that the story of national and constitutional development became really problematic. Yet, Stubbs claimed, out of a dismal story of dynastic bloodshed and cruelty, 'emerges in spite of all, the truer and brighter day, the season of more general conscious life, higher longings, more forbearing, more sympathetic, purer, riper liberty'.[28] The Lancastrians had failed to make a parliamentary monarchy work, and the result was Yorkist and Tudor despotism, but this was not a break with the sacred principle of continuity, for both experiments were 'stages in the discipline of national life … the constitution had in its growth outrun the capacity of the nation; the nation needed rest and renewal, discipline and reformation, before it could enter into the enjoyment of its birthright'.[29] So the nation had needed some hard schooling before it was ready for maturity. Thus, in Stubbs's world, the English nation and the constitution developed together, usually in harmony, or else one had to wait for the other to catch up. It was a sophisticated treatment of a long and complex period, but essentially it was a one-plot story, made respectable by the apparent solidity of documentary evidence, in an era that prized national, political history above all else.

Stubbs's friend, John Richard Green, supplied the popular appeal that Stubbs's weighty three volumes lacked. His *Short History of the English People* (1874) was a huge bestseller, displacing Macaulay. It was translated into many languages, and it sold well in America, not least because in the eyes of the Whig historians, the American War of Independence was explained as the triumph of the English settlers' love of liberty and representative institutions – another apparent discontinuity to be explained away as really the triumph of the very principles that appeared to be being denied.[30] Green supplied the dramatic scenes, the romantic stories that Stubbs's more sober account lacked. For example, after a stirring narration of the landing of Hengest, the first English leader to land in what he and his successors were to turn into England, he painted an entirely imaginary picture of the English war-band breaking out from their bridgehead into their promised land, and linked it to more recent times in a patriotic way:

> The Chronicle of the conquering people tells nothing of the rush that may have carried the ford, or the fight that went struggling up through the village. It only tells that Horsa fell in the moment of victory; and the flint-heap of Horsted, which has long preserved his name, and was held in after-time to mark his grave, is thus the earliest of those monuments of English valour of which Westminster is the last and noblest shrine.[31]

In strictly 'scientific' historical terms, this is of course absolute nonsense, but the romance of it all is supposed to imprint what is, by the admission of the author, make-believe, upon the reader's mind. The deliberate anachronism of linking a legendary association of a pile of stones with the memory of a fallen, and mythical, national hero, and then linking it to Westminster Abbey, where more recent national heroes were honoured, is an example of what, for their critics, was the besetting sin of the progressive Whig view of history. The Whig historians were so keen to trace the origins of their own world, particularly their constitution, that they were constant prey to anachronism, seeing the past through the eyes of the present.

Twilight of the Whigs

By the end of the nineteenth century the more 'professional' historians had become highly critical of this Whig propensity for anachronism and for telling the national story in a liberal, progressive light. They felt that the Whigs had allowed Victorian preconceptions to colour their archival findings, and were determined to erase such an overarching theme from their detailed studies. The *coup de grâce* to the reputation of the Whigs in academia was delivered, rather late in the day, in Herbert Butterfield's *The Whig Interpretation of History* (1931), which made great play with their bias and anachronisms.[32] Butterfield's attack was much applauded at the time, but in due course the sort of professional objectivity that he preached has come to be seen as largely spurious and, in its turn, as merely a product of its own times. Certainly English academic historiography avoided much contact with the world of ideas once a rather stifling concern for minute research and avoiding too much generalisation set in. The only exception was the minority of Marxists in the profession. Many years later, long after Whiggism held the academic stage, a postmodernist writer attacked the notion of continuity. Michel Foucault will have had other more modern metanarratives in mind, when he proclaimed that for postmodernists the discontinuity was important.

> For history in its classical form, the discontinuous was both the given and the unthinkable: the raw material of history, which presented itself in the form of dispersed events – decisions, accidents, initiatives, discoveries; the material, which, through analysis, had to be rearranged, reduced, effaced in order to reveal the continuity of events. Discontinuity was the stigma of temporal dislocation that it was the historian's task to remove from history.[33]

One has to admit, however reluctantly, that that just about sums up Stubbs. Foucault, of course, went on to extol the importance of the discontinuity in historiography.

Why should we concern ourselves with an anachronistic Victorian approach to English history? Firstly, it illustrates the power of contemporary opinion in shaping the attitudes of historians: the same attitudes that shaped Whig attitudes to the Great Reform Act of 1832, and that held moderate reform was necessary to preserve what was good in the parliamentary constitution, shaped historians' attitudes to past events. The same confidence that made Victorians see Britain and its empire as an example to the world, made historians proud of their national history. It is also worth noting that Whig history and the transference of historiography from the literary to the academic world occurred when the Victorians were exceptionally concerned with the phenomenon of time, and everything was seen to have a historical dimension.[34] Secondly, though out of fashion for many years in academic circles, it lived on in the popular mind, even to the extent of affecting the course of events. Winston Churchill, the descendant of John Churchill, the first Duke of Marlborough and Whig hero, was born almost bound to accept a Whig view of history, which affected not only his own historical writing, for which he received a Nobel Prize for literature, but also his own political actions. Who can doubt that his inspirational wartime speeches were seeing the British role in the Second World War in Whig terms, as a fight for freedom and the continuation of the national traditions? Everything he urged the nation to do was in the context of its national history. Even Butterfield, the erstwhile critic of the Whig interpretation, resorted to patriotic Whig histories under the pressure of the War. In the twenty-first century, popular television history provides examples of the tenacity of the Whig approach. In 2004, David Starkey began a long series of programmes on the English monarchy, which, despite its un-Whig but populist title, 'Monarchy', was relentlessly Whig in its approach, presenting the monarchy as the product of the national will and limited by its contractual relationship with the nation and the nation's capacity to win over even its foreign kings.[35] Stubbs and Green would recognise almost everything that Starkey said. Furthermore, modern scholarship, which is not informed by the Whig view of history overall, does still deal with the sort of issues that concerned the Whigs and it is useful to know the historiographical context. To take one obvious example, historians have returned to an interest in how a sense of English nationhood was established in the early middle ages. The motivation was, in part, consequent upon devolution policy in Britain and contemporary concern about Englishness. There was a new desire to examine the issue as part of the wider examination of the other nationalities within Britain and Ireland. Most general studies of nationalism assume it to be a modern phenomenon, often associated in particular with the nineteenth-century nationalist movements.[36] But others consider real ethnic origins to be relevant to modern nationalism.[37] The Whig concern with Anglo-Saxon origins can be seen as part of a typical nineteenth-century concern to find deep roots for a modern sense of nationhood. But some medievalists have again come to discern a sense of national identity even in the early middle ages.[38] However, because of the devolution context, their approach was often in contrast to that of their Victorian predecessors. It also involved considering the importance of myths, of texts and perceptions, rather than concrete realities, discussed more later in Chapter 3, in connection with postmodernism. But the Whig approach is, either explicitly or implicitly, the alternative interpretation that this new scholarship is set against.[39]

The standards of academic history

A series like 'Monarchy' by David Starkey reminds us that, important as academic history is, it exists within a wider sense of the past that is as likely to be derived from television documentaries or from fiction, whether in films, plays or novels. Of course, as with Whig history, the popular story is quite likely to be derived from the academic history of years ago, while the academic world has moved on. This brings us to the question of genre. Within academic history we expect high standards of research and scholarship. Since professionalisation, the conventional way of indicating a well researched piece is through the footnote or endnote. This is supposed to indicate that the work is soundly based on evidence, and that full account has been taken of existing scholarship. To achieve the first objective, the notes must refer to primary sources, such as cabinet minutes or foreign office dispatches, say, for a certain type of political history. To achieve the second, the secondary sources should be cited, either to incorporate the conclusion of the extant scholarship or provide a reasoned explanation for why it can be discounted either in full or in part. For nearly a century, even in Britain with its rather reluctant professionalisation, the Ph.D. has been the model for this type of monograph, as the book based on the specialist research project is sometimes called. The doctorate has sometimes been called the apprentice piece, referring to the old practice of an apprentice having to produce a work of craftsmanship to demonstrate his right of graduation to the guild. The same standards are expected of articles published in the learned journals of the historical profession of which the *English Historical Review* was the first of many in Britain. In fact, some articles are so well footnoted that it has been known for the footnotes to exceed the wordage of the main text. Sometimes, you will find that an article is the first occasion on which a historian has aired a particular interpretation and that a book, taking a broader view of the topic, has followed. There is an unofficial hierarchy of journals; and journals all have their own traditions of what sort of article they publish. Some are, of course, specialist journals as far as topic is concerned, but many have stated, and others have unstated, preferences for the type of argument they want to hear. Publishers, both commercial ones and university presses, can be similarly distinguished. Some academic presses rarely, if ever, get their books into bookshops, relying on purchases from university libraries for their limited sales. A few books transcend the distinction between the bestseller and the academically respectable. A textbook, such as this, does not usually purport to be a work of original scholarship, though it may incorporate earlier research by the authors, but otherwise, if it is aimed at an undergraduate audience, it would be expected to conform to the same academic standards. The popularity of history has led to a blurring of the distinction between the amateur and the professional in recent years: high standards of authentication are generally expected of popular works; some academics have resigned their posts in order to concentrate on their more glamorous, possibly more rewarding, if less secure roles as television presenters or popular authors. Intellectual trading is not all in one direction. Some of the most influential historiography has been from outside the history profession strictly speaking, even if from inside the 'academy'. As Richard J. Evans has observed,[40] E.P. Thompson's *The Making of the English Working Class* (1963) was written by a man with very little experience of working in an academic history department. And Edward Said's *Orientalism* (1978), similarly, was academic, but from an English and Comparative Literature department,[41] not history. Both Thompson's and Said's work had wider political as well as academic significance. The history profession has not been as narrow-minded as some of its critics have made out.

One issue that the reader needs to address is whether the same standards have to be applied to different genres. Certainly they do if works purport to be original interpretations, whoever the authors, be they famous professors, obscure academics, or professional writers. A pot-boiler, which has nothing new to say, will be judged by the appropriate standards: if it says it well and for a different readership, and is not hopelessly outdated or misguided, it can still be valuable. The worst type of publication is outright plagiarism, that is, unacknowledged copying of another's ideas or even words – fortunately rare in published work, though not unknown. The profession tries to keep control of standards in two ways. All journals of any repute employ readers from the academic world to give freely their opinions about articles submitted. Published books are usually reviewed by fellow academics in some of the learned journals. The refereeing of journal articles occasionally becomes front-page news, more usually in the natural sciences or medicine, and the editor of the journal has to explain that the controversial piece has been properly refereed. Only rarely does history hit the headlines in a similar way. It took an ill-judged attempt to sue Penguin Books and Deborah Lipstadt for libel, by David Irving, in the 'Holocaust denial' trial, for history to receive the same level of publicity as an article about the safety of a vaccine.

Reviews should be subject to the same critical consideration as anything else one reads. Who wrote the review and what do we know about that person's position on the topic under discussion? In the academic world there are no professional reviewers, only professional academics, but there are professional rivalries. The arrival of the Internet has introduced a new dimension to historiography. Some historians have set up their own web sites. Just as the printed word has lent a spurious authority to an argument, so the 'information revolution' has given the credulous a belief that 'electronic' information is authoritative, even though mostly it is unmonitored. It is a wise history department that conducts exercises in discriminating use of the Internet, and a wise student that asks exactly what is meant by 'information'.

Postmodernism

By the end of the twentieth century, just when historians thought they knew what professional standards meant, after a century of practice, the postmodernists told them that practices such as referencing were part of a dubious effort to provide authority to an argument when everything was relative.[42] Even the plain language of historical scholarship was part of the deception.[43] Early on in the professionalisation process, Freeman noted that 'history is the least technical of all studies; it is absolutely without technical terms', and jokingly added to a geologist friend who, he said, was making up 'arbitrary' scientific names for his own subject, 'History has no technical terms – I half wish it had, just to frighten away fools'.[44] Over a century later history's dalliance with social science, economics, even philosophy, had rather eroded that early linguistic innocence, but plain English and jargon were both seen as part of the academic effort to achieve a dubious authority.

It is time to take a closer look at postmodernism and its relationship to historiography. 'Compare history to a tree', writes Ankersmit. Those who formed large-scale philosophies of history or historians who wanted to find some principle 'that held everything together in the past' and which was the basis of our understanding of the past, saw history as the trunk of a tree. 'Historism and modernist scientific historiography', to use Ankersmit's formulation for what, in Britain, would have constituted the majority of non-Marxist professional historians, located their 'praiseworthy' attempts to write about 'what in fact happened in the past' without any general presuppositions, in the branches of the tree, but remained interested in the relationship of the branches to the trunk; to the idea of history as a whole in other words, hoping perhaps that ultimately it might be possible to understand it. Postmodernist historiography, however, chooses not the trunk or the branches, but the leaves. 'Within the postmodernist view of history, the goal is no longer integration, synthesis, and totality, but it is those historical scraps which are the centre of attention.' Ankersmit continues:

> Fifteen to twenty years ago we would have asked ourselves in amazement whatever the point could be of this kind of historical writing, what it is trying to prove and this very obvious question would have been prompted then, as it always is, by our modernist desire to get to know how the machine of history works.[45]

Such a question, he adds, has lost its meaning; the leaves of the tree are what historiography is now. Continuing his metaphor, he says that 'autumn has come to Western historiography', detaching the leaves from the tree. The winds of autumn are 'the postmodernist nature of our own time' and 'the changed position of Europe in the world since 1945', which has marginalised the one-time grand narratives, such as the progress of Reason or the struggle of the proletariat – references to Hegelian and Marxist influences. Now the leaves have fallen, we have no interest in where they were on the tree, but can arrange them in whatever pattern we wish. We can make of them what we want. The idea of seeing something in its historical context is finished; we can play with memories but not reconstruct the past.[46]

As an extended metaphor this works better than most. It indicates why postmodernism has both attracted and repelled historians. It has attracted them because, contrary to the belief of postmodernists, many historians, certainly in Britain, have never really signed up to a positivist, scientific ideal of historical knowledge, and have rarely been interested in the whole tree, unless they were Marxists, not since the weakening of the Whig school anyway. Many did not have far to travel to adopt a weak form of postmodernism. The repulsion comes with the relativist notion that we can make our own patterns with the leaves, perhaps for our own amusement, which many historians regard as subverting the historian's purpose of understanding the past.Unlike other '-isms' that have affected history, it is difficult to trace postmodernism back to one source. Most postmodernists recognise the German philosophers, Nietzsche and Heidegger, as forerunners, but it would be an excess of zeal on our part to go back to them here. Leading postmodernist thinkers were mostly French; Jacques Derrida (1930–2004) and Michel Foucault (1926–84) being perhaps the most prominent in historians' minds. Some of their most enthusiastic followers have been American, but since about 1990 the British historical establishment has been influenced and antagonised by postmodernism in equal measure. The suggestion has been made that 'the influence of postmodernism among late-twentieth century historians would have remained entirely marginal – the stuff of philosophical disputation – if the discipline of history had not been changing. Crucial to the change was the entering wedge of relativism and scepticism.'[47] This was an American perspective but it is worth considering whether or not it was true for Western historiography in general, in which case we have, surely, more than a coincidence of a philosophical trend and an historiographical tendency; this would suggest common cultural origins for such a meeting of minds, perhaps – to resurrect an old-fashioned idea – a spirit of the age.

Be that as it may, it is possible to sum up the general effect of 'postmodern' attitudes upon historiography without looking too carefully at the genesis of these ideas. Paradoxically it is best to start with a definition of modernism as postmodernists see it. Modernism is said to have begun with the eighteenth-century Enlightenment which challenged tradition and scripture as the basis for social organisation and belief, and put Reason in their place. The rational individual was going to unlock the secrets of nature through science and, later, the secrets of society through social science; and history was the story of the march of Reason. In principle, everything was capable of analysis and of being understood. Some would associate this modernism with the modernisation of society as well, with man's conquest of nature in the Industrial Revolution, with attempts at social engineering and economic management. Grand themes of social progress informed modernist philosophies like Hegel's or Marx's. Certain branches of history, most noticeably social history in Britain, have been seen by postmodernists as part of the modernist or Enlightenment 'project'. This idea of an Enlightenment 'project' is one of postmodernism's frequently used terms, and seems to suggest attachment to a particular structured view or narrative of recent history, something postmodernists are supposed to be sceptical about.[48]

For scepticism is the hallmark of postmodernism. The ambitions of modernism are seen to be insubstantial. For historiography, the scattered leaves, rearranged at will, have replaced the type of historiography that was part of a project to make sense of the historical process, to focus on the trunk of the tree. There may be an element of cynicism here, arising from disillusionment with certain aspects of modernism, on the Left the apparent failure of Marxism politically, and loss of faith in progress and reason in the aftermath of fascism and other well-publicised horrors. Specifically in Britain, the rise of right-wing politics in the 1970s and 1980s, and the sense of living in a post-industrial world in which the old political and class loyalties meant little, can also be related to enthusiasm for postmodernism.[49] Similar points could be made for several Western countries. But there were philosophical bases for the changes as well. For both Derrida and Foucault, language, far from being the essential tool of human communication and reasoning, was an insurmountable barrier or handicap. There was no necessary relationship between reality and the languages utilised to describe and analyse it.[50] Everything could be deconstructed, even the individual person. Authorial intent was inaccessible or irrelevant.[51] This restricted historians to consideration of texts in a very subjective way – indeed everything was a text, because the idea that we could access the real world of the past was a modernist fallacy.[52] A particular target for deconstructionists was 'class', which had been a fundamental social concept for social historians, certainly in Britain, inspired by Marxist and liberal ideas about society.[53] Out, too, would go the traditional historians' concern with causation.[54] Henceforth, everything would be much less clear-cut, and not based on any sort of material reality, nor part of a continuing story.

Overall, there were two main effects of postmodernism, apart of course from the creation of a determined resistance to its influences.[55] Firstly, there was the tendency to deconstruct the old grand narratives, challenging the cherished ideal of truth and the one-time radical ambitions of Left-leaning social historians, as well as the conservative instincts of those who placed their faith in 'professional' standards. In Chapter 3, we take Patrick Joyce as an exemplar of this role. Secondly, what we might call the extreme faction of postmodernists proclaimed the death of historiography. As this book is intended to be a guide to the continued study of historiography in the context of degrees in history, which are predicated mostly on the assumption that we can study the past as well as historiography, we leave readers to pursue this line of thought elsewhere if they so choose,[56] aware that this may be regarded as unforgiveable by fundamentalists. Our final observation on the subject is that the debate between postmodernists and what, for want of a better term and in conformity with others, we will call traditionalists, has been conducted with ferocity and some personal animosity in some instances.[57] This is not unusual. Contrary to popular imaginings of academic life as lived in ivory towers or beneath dreaming spires, the academic world is at times a ferocious battlefield. But the zeal of postmodernists is surprising in view of their fondness for relativism, ambiguity, and the fluidity of interpretations. What is clear is that historiography reflects the social and intellectual changes of the historians' own times as well as the pressure they feel to try to understand the past.

Further reading

General

Bentley, M. (ed.), *Companion to Historiography* (Routledge, 1997).
Evans, R.J., *In Defence of History* (Granta Books, 1997).

The history of historiography

Burrow, J.W., *A Liberal Descent: Victorian Historians and the English Past*

(Cambridge University Press, 1981).

Iggers, G.G., *The German Conception of History* (Wesleyan University Press, 1983).

Parker, C., *The English Historical Tradition Since 1850* (John Donald, 1990).

Stubbs, W., 'A sketch of the constitutional history of the English nation down to the reign of Edward the first', in Stubbs, *Select Charters and Other Illustrations of English Constitutional History from the Earliest Time to the Reign of Edward the First* (Clarendon Press, 8th edn, 1895), pp. 1–51.

Postmodernism

Appleby, J., L. Hunt and M. Jacob, *Telling the truth about history* (Norton and Co., 1994).

Munslow, A., *Deconstructing History* (Routledge, 1997).

Notes

1 For brief accounts, see R.J. Evans, *In Defence of History* (Granta Books, 1997), pp. 15–23; M. Bentley (ed.), *Companion to Historiography* (Routledge, 1997), pp. 406–8, 419–23. To pursue the subject in more depth, see G.G. Iggers, *The German Conception of History* (Wesleyan University Press, 1983); L. von Ranke, *The Theory and Practice of History* (Bobbs-Merrill, 1973).

2 Iggers, *The German Conception of History*, pp. 63–89.

3 G.P. Gooch, *History and Historians in the Nineteenth Century* (Longmans, 1952), pp. 73, 96–7. *History and Historians* was first published in 1913 and represents a common view of Ranke at the time.

4 Iggers, *The German Conception of History*, pp. 63–5.

5 A. Comte, *The Essential Writings: Auguste Comte and Positivism*, ed. G. Lenger (Transaction Publishers, 1998), pp. 71–2, 75, 195–7.

6 W.R. Keylor, *Academy and Community: The Foundation of the French Historical Profession* (Harvard University Press, 1975).

7 Iggers, *The German Conception of History*, p. 78.

8 C. Parker, *The English Historical Tradition since 1850* (John Donald, 1990), pp. 20–40; C. Parker, 'English Historians and the opposition to Positivism', *History and Theory*, xxii (1983), pp. 120–45.

9 Parker, *The English Historical Tradition since 1850*, pp. 83–101.

10 C. Parker, 'The Development of History Courses in British Universities, 1850–1975', MA Dissertation, Exeter University, 1976, pp. 25–52.

11 The Historical Association was established in 1906, *History* in 1912 and the Institute of Historical Research in 1921. See Parker, *The English Historical Tradition since 1850*, pp. 87–8. For details see: D.S. Goldstein, 'The

organisational development of the British historical profession, 1884–1921',
Bulletin of the Institute of Historical Research, lv 132 (1982), pp. 180–93.

12 Bede, *Ecclesiastical History of the English People with Bede's Letter to Egbert and Cuthbert's Letter on the Death of Bede* (with Introduction by D.H. Farmer) (Penguin Books, 1990), Introduction, pp. 19–35; and pp. 41–74, 186–94.

13 J. Kenyon, *The History Men* (Weidenfeld and Nicolson, 1983), p. 82. For Macaulay's role see pp. 68–84; also see B. Stuchtey, 'Literature, liberty and life of the nation', in S. Berger, M. Donovan and K. Passmore, *Writing National Histories* (Routledge, 1999), pp. 30–43.

14 As late as 1959–60, at one of the 'new civic' universities (Nottingham), one of the authors, as a first-year undergraduate, found himself sitting in a seminar reading 'Stubbs's Charters' in Latin; by then it had become an optional extra; but elsewhere it still held centre-stage.

15 Gooch, *History and Historians in the Nineteenth Century*, pp. 317–34.

16 A key work for further reading on Stubbs (and Macaulay and Freeman) is J.W. Burrow, *A Liberal Descent: Victorian Historians and the English Past* (Cambridge University Press, 1981).

17 W. Stubbs, *Select Charters and Other Illustrations of English Constitutional History from the Earliest Times to the Reign of Edward the First* (Clarendon Press, 8th edn, 1895), pp. 7–8; W. Stubbs, *The Constitutional History of England in its Origin and Development*, Vol. I (Clarendon Press, 2nd edn. 1875), pp. 217, 245–6.

18 Stubbs, *Select Charters*, pp. 1–5; Stubbs, *Constitutional History*, I, pp. 2, 62–5.

19 Stubbs, *Constitutional History*, I, p. iii.

20 Ibid., p. 1.

21 Ibid., pp. 66–8.

22 Ibid., pp. 197–200.

23 C. Parker, 'The failure of liberal racialism: the racial ideas of E.A. Freeman', *Historical Journal*, 24 (1981), pp. 825–46.

24 Stubbs, *Constitutional History*, I, p. 544.

25 Ibid., p. 545.

26 W. Stubbs, *The Constitutional History of England in its Origin and Development*, Vol. II (Clarendon Press, 3rd edn., 1883), p. 103.

27 Ibid., pp. 163–4.

28 Ibid., p. 652.

29 W. Stubbs, *The Constitutional History of England in its Origin and Development*, Vol. III (Clarendon Press, 2nd edn., 1878), p. 286.

30 J.R. Green, *A Short History of the English People* (Macmillan, 1894), pp. 786–7. The greatest advocate of the American War of Independence as

an English triumph was E.A. Freeman; see E.A. Freeman, 'George Washington, the Expander of England', *Greater Greece and Greater Britain; and George Washington, the Expander of England* (Macmillan, 1886), pp. 62–103.

31   Green, *A Short History of the English People*, pp. 7–9.

32   H. Butterfield, *The Whig Interpretation of History* (Penguin Books, 1973).

33   M. Foucault, *The Archaeology of Knowledge* (Tavistock Publications, 1974), p. 8.

34   R. Gilmour, *The Victorian Period: The Intellectual and Cultural Context of English Literature 1830–1890* (Longman, 1993), pp. 25–62.

35   David Starkey, 'Monarchy', Channel 4: 18, 25 October, 1, 8, 15, 22 November, 2004.

36   S. Berger, 'National Movements', in S. Berger (ed.). *A Companion to Nineteenth-Century Europe 1789–1914* (Blackwell, 2006), pp. 178–92; E.J. Hobsbawm, *Nations and Nationalism since 1780: Programme, Myth, Reality* (Cambridge University Press, 1990); J. Breuilly, *Nationalism and the State* (Manchester University Press, 1993); B. Anderson, *Imagined Communities: Reflections on the Origin and Spread of Nationalism* (Verso, 1991).

37   A.D. Smith, *The Ethnic Origin of Nations* (Blackwell, 1986).

38   H. Schulze, *States, Nations and Nationalism: From the Middle Ages to the Present* (Blackwell, 1998).

39   R.R. Davies, *The First English Empire: Power and Identity in the British Isles 1093–1343* (Oxford University Press, 2000); see also a series of Presidential Addresses by R.R. Davies to the Royal Historical Society, *Transactions of the Royal Historical Society* (*TRHS*), published in 1994–97; S. Foot, 'The making of angelcynn: English identity before the Norman Conquest', *TRHS*, vi (1996), pp. 25–49; and J.L. Nelson, 'Presidential Address: England and the continent in the ninth century: II the Vikings and others', *TRHS*, xiii (2003), pp. 1–28. For a review of Stubbs's role see J. Campbell, 'Stubbs and the English State', in J. Campbell, *The Anglo-Saxon State* (Hambledon and London, 2000), pp. 248–68.

40   Evans, *In Defence of History*, p. 208.

41   Both books will be referred to further in Chapter 3.

42   G.M. Spiegel, 'History, historicism and the social logic of the text in the middle ages', *Speculum*, lxv (1990), p. 64; J. Habermas, *The Philosophical Discourse of Modernity* (Polity Press, 1987), p. 250. See also M. Foucault, *The Archaeology of Knowledge* (Tavistock Publications, 1974), pp. 6–7, 10–11; A. Munslow, *Deconstructing History* (Routledge, 1997), p. 122.

43   S. Cohen, *Historical Culture: On the Recoding of an Academic Discipline* (University of California Press, 1986), p. 2.

44 E.A. Freeman, *The Methods of Historical Study: Eight Lectures, Read in the University of Oxford in Michaelmas Term, 1884* (Macmillan, 1886), pp. 93–4; W.R.W. Stephens, *The Life and Letters of Edward A. Freeman*, 2 vols (Macmillan, 1895), ii, pp. 195, 202.

45 F. Ankersmit, 'Historiography and Postmodernism', *History and Theory*, 28 (1989), pp. 148–9.

46 Ibid.

47 J. Appleby, L. Hunt, M. Jacob, *Telling the Truth about History* (Norton and Co., 1994), p. 216.

48 E. Breisach, *On the Future of History* (University of Chicago Press, 2003), pp. 11–14; J. Appleby et al., *Telling the Truth about History*, pp. 201–5.

49 M. Bentley (ed.), *Companion to Historiography* (Routledge, 1997), pp. 488–9; D. McLellan, *Ideology* (Open University Press, 1995), pp. 73–4; and specifically in relation to class see P. Joyce, *Democratic Subjects: The Self and the Social in Nineteenth-century England* (Cambridge University Press, 1994), pp. 2–3.

50 J. Appleby et al., *Telling the Truth about History*, pp. 213–15, 266–7.

51 Ibid., pp. 202–16; Breisach, *On the Future of History*, pp. 154–7; P. Joyce, 'The end of social history?', *Social History*, 20:1 (1995), p. 83.

52 G. Spiegel, 'History, historicism and the social logic of the text in the middle ages', *Speculum*, lxv (1990), pp. 63, 69.

53 Joyce, 'The end of social history?', pp. 73–91. Joyce's work will be examined in Chapter 3.

54 Evans, *In Defence of History*, pp. 138–40.

55 Breisach, *On the Future of History*, pp. 117–22; Evans, *In Defence of History*. Despite the bitterness of Keith Jenkins's response to Evans, *In Defence of History* is not an unthinking 'traditionalist' reaction to postmodernism.

56 Breisach, *On the Future of History*, pp. 116–17; M. Fulbrook, *Historical Theory* (Routledge, 2002), pp. 18–20.

57 On the extreme postmodernist front: K. Jenkins, *Why history? Ethics and Postmodernism* (Routledge, 1999), pp. 95–114; for the 'revisionist' postmodernists, Joyce, 'The end of social history?', pp. 77–8; for the 'traditionalists', G.R. Elton, *Return to Essentials* (Cambridge University Press, 1991), pp. 27–49, 58–61.

3

Engaging with historiography

In Chapter 2 we looked at academic historiography as the context in which most recent works of historical scholarship have to be assessed. In this chapter we provide a guide to reading those texts. As before, we will illustrate the arguments with historiographical examples.

Facts and theories

As we have seen, there have been a number of schools of history in different places at different times. Some have been naive in the sense that they represented the conventional views of the age or of a particular educated social group, which may have been conscious of its own predilections, but not have been aware of subscribing to a particular philosophy of history or of being biased towards a particular interpretation. They would often regard themselves as being objective and professional, perhaps even scientific, depending on their attitude to such a term. The English tradition of the Whig interpretation is an example of this type.

Other schools of history have been overtly dedicated to an overall philosophy of history, of how we know the past and by what general principles the process of historical change takes place. The Annales school, in France, is an obvious case. When Marc Bloch and Lucien Febvre founded the journal *Annales d'histoire économique et sociale* in 1929 they had a clear mission to develop a new type of history, less based on narratives of events, more influenced by social science; less concerned with the supposedly shallow effect of politics and more interested in structural social and economic change and continuity. After the Second World War, the change of title of the journal to *Annales: économies sociétés, civilisations* signified an increasingly structuralist approach as well as a new emphasis on cultures. From the 1960s and 1970s onwards, the school had widespread influence in the English-speaking academic world, when the work of Fernand Braudel and then Le Roy Ladurie, especially, was translated.[1] Marxist historians, with their belief in historical materialism, are another example of an overt school of history. Though Marxism eventually showed signs of factional disputes, they had a fundamental belief that the predominant factor in history was the economic structure of society, its way of getting a living, of subsisting: all other aspects of human behaviour were affected by this material consideration. The most fundamental argument within the Marxist tradition has been about whether or not this constitutes economic determinism. Moreover, the ownership of property within a given economic system, be it feudalism or capitalism, determined class structure; change came when the system of production changed. Marxists can trace the ancestry of their ideas, even when in dispute with each other, back to Marx himself. At most times, they have had a greater tendency than their fellow academics to want to put their ideas into political action. They certainly constitute a self-conscious school of history.[2]

Philosophers of history tend to be critical of the naive type of school, arguing that the greatest dangers to objectivity come from those who think they are objective but are insufficiently aware of their own presumptions.[3] Historians who believe themselves to be free of bias are usually most critical of those they think are dominated by what they call 'theory'. Their argument is that theory-led historians know what they want to find in the archives and, of course, cannot fail to find it, being blind to other evidence or to other interpretations, blind to what their critics call the 'facts'. One of the most outspoken critics of what he called thesis-led historiography was G.R. Elton, who argued that properly professional historians approached the archives without preconceptions or even questions in mind.[4] On a commonsense principle, one would expect historians always to be ready to renounce a theory, had they been unwise enough to get entangled in one, in favour of the facts. But what exactly are these facts to which historians are traditionally so attached?An examination of any historical controversy will quickly establish that there is no sharp dividing line between fact and theory. Moving beyond the simple fact of, for example, somebody's date of birth or place of birth, to something that has more meaning, that is, to a higher level fact, we find that a fact is itself a kind of theory, a construction, that we have decided to accept as true. If, instead of the birth of an individual person, we are talking of, say, the birth of a class, then clearly what is a fact for some is an unacceptable theory for others. The evidence that E.P. Thompson produced for *The Making of the English Working Class*, even though it has been part challenged by his critics,[5] is generally accepted as true, but his conclusion still divides opinion. According to Thompson, the English working class made itself, roughly between 1780 and 1832. It was not made by the Industrial Revolution or the capitalist class which provided employment in the workplaces. Classes came into existence through class struggle.[6] According to some of his critics on the left, Thompson had abandoned the true theory of Marxism. According to right-wing critics he had allowed his interpretation of the facts to be dictated by preconceived theory. For those who like to keep their ideas simple, Thompson was offering an interpretation that was worryingly complex yet difficult to delimit. In place of the working class being created by being forced into proletarianisation by the middle classes of the Industrial Revolution, and then acquiring class-consciousness, came the idea of class struggle without class – seemingly an oxymoron – and a 'cultural' interpretation, as opposed to a narrowly economic one of how classes were formed. But worse was to come. Though Thompson's approach[7] dominated all discussion of the subject for about thirty years, by the 1990s some historians influenced by postmodernist ideas, and some would say poststructuralism, began to question not only Thompson's conclusions but the dominance of class as an issue. The work of Patrick Joyce is an important example of the new mood.

'Class' and Patrick Joyce

In *Visions of the People* (1991)[8] and *Democratic Subjects* (1994)[9], Joyce questioned both Thompson's assertion that the working class was made, or rather made itself, by 1830, and the extent to which people defined themselves by class. His ideas are complex, but perhaps they are most accessible in his introduction to *Class* (1995) in the 'Oxford Readers' series. Here he admitted that one of the reasons why 'class' had become less powerful as an organising concept was that it no longer looked appropriate for the 1990s:

> In recent years the concept of class has come under increasing scrutiny as a means of explaining both the present and the past. The reasons for this lie in the profound economic, political, and intellectual changes marking our time. Class is seen by some to be unequal to the task of explaining our present reality. And this view has been of great effect among historians too: if class fails to interpret the present, perhaps it has not given an adequate account of our past either?[10]

The destruction of old heavy industries, the rise of modern communications, the intellectual impact of the collapse of the Soviet Union, the success of right-wing governments in the 1980s and the rise of poststructuralism and postmodernism were all seen to have created a new world where class no longer seemed so real or, at least, dominant. New concepts of self, and feminism, also helped to make class suspect not just in the contemporary world but as a tool of historical analysis as well.[11] As Joyce then put it, 'Once the idea of "class consciousness" as a unitary, coherent form of identity is questioned, then the matter of multiple identities and the relationships between them becomes apparent (alongside class we have "people", gender, and so on)'.[12] There was a time when historians who challenged Thompson's definition of class, even though it had been informed by historiographical and political traditions quite different from narrow economistic Marxism, would have revelled in the supposed triumph of empirical evidence successfully challenging a theory-based interpretation. But not Joyce. He does not just discard earlier interpretations of class; he does not claim that the facts have triumphed over theory. He admits that new perspectives are changing the way we view things. Joyce's *Democratic Subjects* provides us with an illustration. The new perspective has allowed 'other forms of the self and of collective identity' to emerge, forms 'long obscured by the concentration on class. And class itself, like any other collective "social" subject, is seem to be an imagined form, not something given in a "real" world beyond this form.' This could almost be taken as a *leitmotiv* for postmodernism, at least when it undertakes to write history as opposed to denying it. Joyce is undertaking to examine the social or collective selves that had, he argues, 'more significance than class at the time', and were represented by terms like 'the people', 'humanity' or 'mankind'; and he includes the term 'democratic' in the list of attributes with which people identified. This could only be done by accepting that these were 'imagined' allegiances.[13] It is important to stress that these are imagined communities in the sense they exist in the minds of the people, not imaginary in the sense of being invented by the historian. They are seen to be more real than any supposedly objective, material structured reality based upon economic exploitation. It could be argued that this only completes the journey begun when Thompson rejected economic determinism and opted for a 'cultural' explanation of class, but Joyce argues that there is an important distinction to be made between putting 'culture' at the end of the argument and insisting that 'experience' and 'productive relations' themselves can only be understood through the 'imaginary'.[14]

The influence of postmodernism can often be discerned from the titles and the topics chosen by authors. Joyce, for example, chose *Visions of the People* as carefully as he chose *Democratic Subjects*. 'Visions' involve envisioning both of and by the people, and have connotations of imagination, dreams, prophecy, hope and desire.[15] But, above all, they are imagined, and it often easy to spot the retreat from confident materialism in postmodern titles. *Visions of the People* is perhaps almost transitional in that Joyce does raise the possibility that class as dominant master narrative may have been only deferred. Far from the working class being self-made by 1830, he suggests that even his own period, 1848–1914, had not seen the whole story. A sense of class became, perhaps, more evident after 1914.[16] This is the sort of conclusion that could be tested, albeit never with a sense that such a complex social phenomenon could be subjected to universally agreed objective criteria. But Thompson's conclusion that the working class had made itself by 1830 and Joyce's suggestion that a sense of class, having shared its power with many other visions, was only coming into its own after 1914, cannot really be reconciled. In theory at least, research could settle the argument; the 'facts' could show that either Thompson's Marxist-derived, if transmuted, theories, or Joyce's poststructuralist ideas were incompatible with the evidence. But of course the importance of the postmodernists' critique of earlier notions of class goes far beyond that; they are indeed envisioning things differently, and a simplistic distinction between 'fact' and 'theory' will not suffice. If we wish to take seriously the conclusions drawn by historians, whether they be in the mould of E.P. Thompson or Patrick Joyce, we have to consider what Oakeshott said about facts. According to Oakeshott, the historian, even if free from 'mere prejudice and preconception', starts with some postulates and a hypothesis, but ends with facts: 'history, like every other form of thought, ends and does not begin with facts'.[17] This certainly applies to what we might call higher level facts – the theories that historians have come to believe must be accepted.

Class and the French Revolution

This is not to say that one interpretation is necessarily as good as another or that every interpretation is true for its own generation. Take the argument that raged about the origins of the French Revolution for approximately forty years after the Second World War. Here once again, a Marxist interpretation is being challenged. Many would regard the success of Alfred Cobban in challenging the Marxist interpretation of the French Revolution as put forward by Georges Lefebvre as a triumph of English empiricism over French Marxism. Cobban certainly saw it that way:

> One object of this study (*The Social Interpretation of the French Revolution*, first published in 1964) has been to suggest, by providing a positive example, the possibility of an empirical approach to the writing of social history, which will enable it to escape from the rigid patterns of system-makers who have deduced their history from their theories.[18]

Though this empiricist critique is very different in its approach to a postmodernist one, we might note some parallels: both, in their different ways, are deconstructing a materialist approach to social structure and both regard language as a key issue; in attempting to understand the past both want to use the language of the past as opposed to that of ahistorical social theory. Largely because of this dispute, studies of the French Revolution are some of the most methodologically explicit since Cobban's attack. Lefebvre's interpretation, translated into English as *The Coming of the French Revolution*, was in essence that the revolution was caused by the rise of the bourgeoisie, and therefore he provided Marxism with an example of social and political change coming about as a result of the changes that had occurred in the social or productive relations that had hitherto been feudal in character and had now become capitalist. Similarly, Christopher Hill characterised the English Civil War as a bourgeois revolution. Not that Lefebvre's interpretation was simplistic or deterministic. As Doyle has put it, paraphrasing Lefebvre:

> Yet there was nothing automatic in this development, at least in the short run. The bourgeoisie were able to overthrow the aristocracy because the political authority of the monarchy had collapsed. It had collapsed because the monarchy was unable to pay its way. And it was unable to pay its way because the aristocracy, the 'privileged orders' of nobility and clergy, clung to their exemptions and privileges, and used their political power to prevent the king from making the necessary reforms.[19]

The above is a splendid example, albeit a paraphrase and synopsis, of the sort of history that sought to explain events, an approach less fashionable in the early twenty-first century. But even this concurrence of events might not have been enough to secure the victory of the bourgeoisie. Having been roused by the nobility, the bourgeoisie in turn called on the urban poor, the populace of Paris; and then a peasant revolt destroyed the feudal order in the country. Four revolutions for the price of one, but of course the bourgeoisie were the ultimate beneficiaries; it was their historic moment. This was a neat explanation that, none the less, avoided a simplistic overly-economistic approach.

Cobban was able to destroy it by the simple device of showing that the 'revolutionary bourgeois' were not the rising capitalist class of merchants and entrepreneurs, the classic bourgeoisie of Marxist analysis, but an endangered section of the middle classes who constituted the lawyers, members of the liberal professions, and holders of minor offices of state which had to be bought but had become unprofitable. The revolution, in other words, was carried out and eventually controlled by men who were opposed to the rising bourgeoisie who were changing the French economy. However, this was not quite the triumph of diligent English empiricism over French theorising as it is usually portrayed. For Cobban drew not only on his own research but on the researches of many French experts including Lefebvre himself. In fact, Lefebvre had also concluded, in 1951, that the businessmen were not the prime movers in the Revolution, but that these minor officials and members of the liberal profession were.[20] So the real difference between Cobban and Lefebvre is that Lefebvre did not recognise the significance for his Marxist metanarrative of this conclusion, whereas Cobban delighted in it.

Revealingly, Lefebvre had already retreated to a position where the significance of the French Revolution, in Marxist terms, had to be maintained by arguing that a bourgeois revolution had still occurred because, though the bourgeoisie had not caused it, they had benefited from it. Cobban then pursued the argument and showed that neither had the French economy nor had the industrial bourgeoisie benefited from, or been transformed by, the Revolution and its aftermath.[21] But in truth, even if Cobban had failed to prove the second part of his argument, the game was up for Lefebvre's interpretation as a Marxist one. For, according to some interpretations, Marxism would have required the change in the productive relations to have preceded the political changes, and Lefebvre had already stood his original argument on its head. In some ways this is even more revealing than the straightforward notion of a clash between a priori theorising and empirical research because it seems that Lefebvre's research did show the flaws in his own thesis, but he was reluctant to see the full consequences for the Marxist narrative. Equally, of course, it could be argued that

Cobban's determined empiricism predisposed his own approach, but on this occasion it allowed him to see more clearly.

The dispute defined the terms of reference for much subsequent research on the Revolution, especially in Britain, but also in France where Albert Soboul took up the Marxist standard. However, a determinedly anti-Marxist French historian, François Furet, was to change the terms of reference.[22] Whereas Cobban debated with Lefebvre and Soboul on their own terms, Furet wrote about the Revolution as an ideology, not as the product of material class interest, nor as the implementation of material sectional interests.[23] He was critical of the concept of causation on the grounds that the Revolution developed its own dynamic, and said that the historiography of the French Revolution had lagged behind other areas in the recognition that facts did not speak for themselves.[24] Since Furet, the old issues of class and material interest have faded and cultural history with a strong interest in personal experience and a relativist approach has come to the fore. Simon Schama's *Citizens*, for example, was conceived as a study, of 'contingencies and unforeseen consequences'[25] far removed from the old notion of structural change. The book is a series of vignettes, character sketches, many of them of hitherto quite obscure participants. As Gildea's *The Past in French History* (1994) exemplifies, interest has shifted to a consideration of the myth and symbolic significance of the Revolution, a shift which the centenary celebrations in 1989 encouraged. Criticising earlier approaches, including an early work of his own, Gildea complained about 'mechanical and deterministic' methods that 'allowed no space between the actors and their past for any relation that was open, playful or in any way problematic'.[26] He set out to look at the role of collective memory in political culture, and of course precisely because of the French Revolution and its long aftermath, there are several collective memories and, therefore, political cultures in France.[27] This, however, led him to a radical conclusion, which though it could be argued should not be taken out of context, nevertheless sounds rather sweeping:

> There can be no objective, universally agreed history, and even if it were possible, it would be of scant interest. What matters is myth, not

in the sense of fiction, but in the sense of a construction of the past, elaborated by a political community for its own ends.[28]

Such a highly relativist position may look extreme to some historians, even if they would accept it in the context of Gildea's particular task, but of course many postmodernists would apply this principle to all historical study. Clearly the French Revolution as a subject of historical study has been moved on from the debate about its role as a 'bourgeois revolution', supposedly capable of being settled by clear-eyed research. The change is even more striking than the change in studies of 'class' in British history. There are only competing narratives and, certainly, no master metanarrative.

Metanarrative

The examples we have chosen to illustrate the problems inherent in the idea of there being an easy distinction between fact and theory, have both been about class and Marxist interpretation of the role of class in the course of history. Marxists have what is sometimes called a metanarrative, that is an overall interpretation of the dynamics behind the course of history or at least a large portion of it. For some people, the metanarrative is the ultimate in misguided, or perhaps one should say misguiding, theory, whether it be Whig progressivism, Marxist dialectics or modernisation theory. Postmodernists, as well as empiricists, have been particularly sceptical about metanarrative.In favour of metanarrative we could argue that it gives a structure to research, and, psychologically, it has appeal because, it has been said, it gives direction and purpose to the course of human history and to its study. Even Karl Popper, a keen opponent of metahistory, recognised its psychological appeal; he felt that it fulfilled an emotional need, being a prediction of change in an otherwise unstable world.[29] Popper designated a belief in laws of historical development or destiny as 'historicism', a rather confusing word, for previously it had been used as a translation of a German term meaning simply a historical approach to explanation, rather in the Rankean manner, a usage far removed from Popper's. It has been suggested that the two usages should be disassociated by using 'historicism' only in the

Popperian and 'historism' in the Rankean sense.[30] Additional to Popper's point, it is also true that there is a strong human desire to order things as well as to explain. However, historiographically and philosophically, metanarrative has been out of fashion since the decline of Marxism from about 1980, and before that one would have to go back to Hegel for a major philosophy based on a historical metanarrative. Hegel's interpretation of history was based on the a priori, or, in his term, 'philosophical' grounds that 'there is Reason in history',[31] and that through the nation state an increasingly rational and free world would emerge. For Hegel, reason and freedom were coterminous. Once these principles had been established, his course of lectures on the philosophy of history fleshed out the actual way in which these principles were realised.[32]

Since the mid-nineteenth century metanarratives have been less in evidence. Sometimes, however, what people write, especially if it is on some large topic, can be infused with an assumption about the course of history that shows a residual metanarrative. The simplest, vaguest and most popular metanarrative has been a belief in progress. With a capital 'P' it usually signifies something metaphysical, maybe in the Hegelian mode, but it can also be a belief in a scientific or technological basis for progress. Occasionally, it can be seen as something that has been historically demonstrable but fortuitous and by no means guaranteed in the future. The most famous pessimistic version of this approach, denying any plot or plan to history, was H.A.L. Fisher in 1934, depressed by the aftermath of the First World War and the decline of liberalism:

> Men wiser and more learned than I have discerned in history a plot, a rhythm, a predetermined pattern. These harmonies are concealed from me. I can see only one emergency following upon another as wave follows upon wave, only one great fact with respect to which, since it is unique, there can be no generalisation, only one safe rule for the historian: that he should recognise in the development of human destinies the play of the contingent and the unforeseen. This is not a doctrine of cynicism and despair. The fact of progress is written plain and large on the page of history, but progress is not a law of nature. The ground gained by one generation may be lost by the next. The thoughts of men may flow into the channels which lead to disaster and barbarism.[33]

With its plangent elegance, this passage was once much quoted by historians and even philosophers, till it became almost a cliché.

In some ways modernisation theory can be seen as a limited version of progress, confining progression to a modern era, once traditional, custom-bound society had given way to modernisation. This could be seen as an American version of the Whig interpretation; more materialistic, but charting the progress of other societies as they emulated American dynamism. Globalisation can be seen as a closely related theme. Imperialism, once in danger of looking outmoded as a topic, as the formal European colonial empires collapsed, when viewed as part of the globalisation process retains its contemporary significance. This is particularly so when, in the wake of British historians' analyses of informal empire alongside formal control, including in 'empire' areas of influence through investment and commerce as opposed to full-scale political control and military occupation or settlement,[34] we can identify the American empire as the successor to the Europeans', and particularly to the British empire. Americans, with their legacy of anti-colonialism arising from their own War of Independence against Britain, have been reluctant to accept that there is such a thing, but with an increase in American military activity on a global scale after the first Gulf War, they became more willing to see that economic penetration also has an imperial dimension. Imperialism thus retains its interest literally on a global scale.

Gentlemanly capitalists?

One of the most influential theses about imperialism, that of Cain and Hopkins in their two-volume *British Imperialism* (1993),[35] fits ideally into a wider narrative of globalisation.[36] The Cain and Hopkins thesis set an agenda for debate.[37] Cain and Hopkins did not suddenly alight upon their thesis in the 1990s; it had been developed in earlier works from the 1970s onwards. In essence, the Cain-Hopkins thesis states that investment overseas was the source of British imperial expansion, that it was the work of the 'gentlemanly' capitalists of the 'City', in London, who preferred 'informal' Empire to outright control. This is not the place for a detailed exposition or analysis of Cain and Hopkins's wide-ranging, well-documented and sophisticated thesis, with its implications for British domestic history as well as imperial history. This can be found in A. Webster's *The Debate on the Rise of the British Empire* in the Manchester University Press 'Issues in Historiography' series. Only one aspect of the many points of significance in the thesis concerns us here: its theme can be subsumed under the general narrative of globalisation, which itself has now acquired a mixed baggage. Investors from the City of London played the key role in establishing a global economy. With this economy go much debated benefits and dangers. Competing visions of the global future, economically, politically, ecologically, and in terms of national and even personal security, confront the world.

However, in one respect at least the Cain-Hopkins thesis looks old-fashioned, despite generating a great debate; and perhaps its lengthy genesis explains this. This is not intended in any way as a criticism of their scholarship or the importance of what they have set out to do. It refers more to changing fashions. They sought to explain a global phenomenon and to do this they were able to relate it to an even wider narrative. Cain and Hopkins later admitted to having been unfashionable: 'Had we given full weight to the influences of the day, we would have had to shift the basis of our work from economic to social and then to cultural history, and to assimilate in turn Marxists, Annalistes and postmodernists.'[38] Intellectually, their book may have looked unfashionable, but it aroused much interest and debate because it addressed the issues of globalisation and Britain's economic performance, subjects of great contemporary interest. As we have seen with some of our other examples, this sort of explanation has often been replaced by work which deals much more with the experience of those involved, with the language of that experience, and eschews the search for causes. Perhaps the best example of such an approach in the field of imperial history is David Cannadine's *Ornamentalism: How the British Saw their Empire*, the clue to the approach being in the subtitle, and recognisable as similar to some of the explicitly postmodern approaches adopted in the other areas of historical scholarship. Cannadine clearly has doubts about postmodernism, reporting that it is often attacked for its 'tortured prose' and 'sketchy' historical knowledge,[39] and who could doubt that those charges can often be made to stick? But his deliberate avoidance of what he calls 'grand narratives', his often ironic style, his frequent qualifications of his general thesis, as well as his concern with, as he often puts it, what the empire 'actually looked like' to the British who ruled it, show that these attitudes are not confined to a narrow group of avowed postmodernists.[40] So too does his abandonment of the profession's traditional practice of hiding the authorial voice in an attempt to create a sense of objectivity. It is typical of his era that Cannadine feels quite happy to include an autobiographical essay explaining how his childhood helped to develop his interest in the British Empire.[41]

Cannadine's particular interest is the way the honours system and the institution of monarchy were used to either replicate, or establish 'analogues' of the social hierarchy of Britain throughout the Empire; replication, or export, to the settlement dominions; and analogues in India, the Crown colonies and the later mandates, concluding in relation to the latter that whether or not the First World War had made the world safe for democracy, as the Allies had boasted, for a generation at least it had 'made the British Empire safe for hierarchy'.[42] In the end, however, his theme leads him to stress the discontinuity at the end of the Empire, as the Indian princes and the rest were abandoned by their British associates,[43] which, of course, is in marked contrast to the 'grand narrative' of historians who see British (and European) imperialism as part of a grander narrative of globalisation. We see that perspective and choice of theme are everything in terms of a relationship to metanarrative. Because of the association of long-scale narratives with overarching schemes of history that assume philosophical and ideological status there has been a tendency for their protagonists to claim scientific, objective status for their narratives; Marxism is perhaps the classic example, though Hegel claimed to have an a priori basis for his philosophy of history. But if one chooses not to write about the state as the embodiment of Reason and the path to Freedom, or about productive relations as the basis of all else, then their philosophies of history can be seen to be merely capricious choices. Cain and Hopkins on the one hand, and Cannadine on the other, are not so much disagreeing with each other as writing from totally different perspectives, with different purposes, even though they share a common topic, the British Empire. But, before we leave Cannadine's *Ornamentalism* we need to see that his choice of title was as significant as his choice of subtitle. To most readers it would be immediately reminiscent of Edward Said's *Orientalism*, first published in 1978 and much reprinted. *Orientalism* is about how western scholars and intellectuals, particularly in France and Britain, categorised the Orient and misrepresented it, indulging in something that was far from 'an innocent scholarly endeavour' but becoming 'an accomplice to empire'.[44] Clearly this view of 'Orientalism' as an imperialist-related mindset which insisted on the otherness of the Islamic world especially, can be seen to conflict with Cannadine's view that the rulers of the British Empire sought analogues with their own hierarchical society.

Francis Fukuyama and others

Before we leave the subject of metanarrative, we should have a brief look at Fukuyama's attempt to revive metanarrative. *The End of History and the Last Man* (1992), which fleshed out and qualified an argument Francis Fukuyama had developed in brief in an earlier work, used the full philosophical apparatus of Hegel and others to argue that history, in the sense of meaningful change and development, had come to an end. There would, of course, be plenty of future events, but the whole world had accepted western democracy and free market capitalism as the practical and ideal way forward. He started to hedge his bets, with qualifications about the possibility of irrational behaviour, also based upon Hegelian notions, but resistance to these twin ideals, such as Islamic fundamentalism, he dismissed as doomed to irrelevance in the long term.[45] Whether viewed as post-Cold War triumphalism, which Fukuyama, an ex-State Department employee, always denied, or dismissed as a shallow attempt to update Hegel, substituting American democracy for the Prussian state as the most rational end-product of history, this metanarrative excited interest, especially in the United States, for a while. It has even been linked to postmodernism because both extreme postmodernists and Fukuyama proclaimed the 'end of history'. But, of course, in seeking to put an overall goal or purpose back into history, Fukuyama was completely at odds with postmodernism, which always rejects metanarrative. *The End of History* does have a superficial appeal, but it is against the tenor of the times, and we do not anticipate that a school of history will follow in Fukuyama's footsteps. In any case, there was competition, albeit without the philosophy Fukuyama used to buttress his argument. Huntington's *The Clash of Civilizations*, which also started life as an article and grew into a book, sees the world as divided by its major 'civilisations', in which religion usually plays a major role; and he counsels against 'the West', for which read the United States, assuming that its aims and ideals can ever be universally accepted.[46] He does not predict the future, but he sketches a worst-case scenario of global conflict. Contemporary concern with environmental degradation has also produced works which see mankind's management of the environment as the key to human success or failure.[47] Here the worst-case scenario is global extinction. We live in an apocalyptic age. But this proliferation of metahistory suggests that their authors have selected their themes rather than observed an objective reality about the fundamental nature of human history. Metahistory is a matter of choice. It is time to turn to the relationship between the standard narrative form and the nature of historical explanation.

Historical explanation

Historians can be excused for feeling very ambivalent about the relationship between narrative and historical explanation. As students, we were often advised to avoid narrative as a form of explanation, and as tutors we are aware of the dangers inherent in slipping uncritically into a narrative, particularly of a biographical kind, when we have been expecting students to display analytical skills in the essays they write or the examination questions they answer. 'Answer the question!' has been the exasperated annotation appearing on many a script over the years. Narrative often appears to be the lazy way of avoiding a selection of material or the application of reason to a historical problem. Similarly, students will often feel a sense of frustration when faced with an analytical question coupled with a long reading list of largely narrative accounts from which they have the task of selecting relevant material. Why, they might reasonably ask, is there a mismatch between what is expected of them for educational purposes and the historiographical form in which researchers often present their findings?

Furthermore, Hayden White has argued that all history is presented in a literary form according to certain classical plot structures: 'narrative accounts of real events admit of as many plot structures as are available'.[48] This might well make the historian feel helpless, in thrall to some inescapable urge to emplotment which has nothing to do with an actual course of events. That historians do use classical plot structures is well illustrated by a popular book on a popular subject by an acknowledged expert in the field: Ian Kershaw has entitled his bestselling two-volume biography of Hitler, *Hitler 1889–1936: Hubris* and *Hitler 1936–1945: Nemesis*,[49] thus utilising the classical Greek concept of – to put it in the vernacular – pride going before a fall, technically a tragic story. But other voices tell us that we need not feel embarrassed about narrative, because our social life is narrativised and, therefore, there need be no distinction between actual social life and narrative: this is the position of Patrick Joyce, for example, in *Democratic Subjects*, dealing with what he calls 'democratic romances'. Narrative gives people purpose, motion and direction.[50] And, from a different philosophical direction, Oakeshott decided that the narrative was a true historical form of explanation. He did not think this because of the actuality of the course of events, for this could never be recaptured. The historians created their own narratives.[51] The term usually used by philosophers of history to describe such a view is 'constructionist', as opposed to those who believe they can 'reconstruct' an actual past or course of events.

Narration can be taken to imply a causal connection between events that are narrated consecutively. The analogy often used is of the snooker cue hitting the cue ball, which strikes another ball, which is in turn pocketed. But rarely does a social situation correspond to a snooker table. Thomas Carlyle summed it up neatly: 'Narrative is linear, Action is solid.' Causal chains are misleading because of the complexity of things.[52] Yet there is something seemingly natural and inherent in narrative: we habitually resort to it in everyday life; in books and in drama (stage, television and film) it is a major source of entertainment although some writers and directors do experiment with the narrative form.[53] But what to put in and what to leave out? How to change the 'solid' social situation into a linear narrative? Clearly selection has to occur or we would begin every account with the emergence of *homo sapiens* and account for every aspect of the creation of the social, political and natural environment in which the event under consideration happened. So even the simplest narrative has to employ a critical intelligence. A successful narrative always has to have an analytical structure as well; and, in historiography, an analytical approach has an implied narrative, if it is to have any meaning.

This brings us to the problem of causation. Philosophers like to distinguish between necessary and sufficient conditions. A necessary condition is one without which something will not occur: combustion will not occur without the presence of oxygen, but oxygen is not a sufficient cause of a fire; a sufficient condition is one which will produce the something under consideration. Most necessary conditions cannot be considered by historians. Nobody could take seriously an explanation of the French Revolution that set out to show that the presence of human beings in France in 1789 was a necessary condition of revolution. Historians have to make a judgement about what conditions need explaining; this is a subjective human judgement about human situations. History, in the sense of historiography, is, in the words of E.H. Carr, 'a process of selection in terms of historical significance ... Just as from the infinite ocean of facts the historian selects those which are significant for his purpose, so from the multiplicity of sequences of cause and effect he extracts those, and only those, which are historically significant; and the standard of historical significance is his ability to fit them into his pattern of rational explanation and interpretation.' Carr was talking about the issue of chance in history and discounting so-called chance considerations as worthy of historical examination, because 'the historian can do nothing with it; it is not amenable to rational interpretation'.[54] But his words are also relevant to all processes of selecting material for historical studies. As the philosopher F.H. Bradley put it, all history was critical history because the historian had to be selective and, therefore, had to have some criterion for selecting material. However, whereas for Carr the criterion was 'historical significance' determined by whether or not it could become part of a rational explanation, for Bradley the criterion could only be the historian's own 'standpoint' or own self, an unacceptably subjective position it would seem, until one realises that only the ideal historian, 'the historian as he ought to be' was the ideal criterion. In reality we could not escape from our imperfect selves, but still we had to be consistent, true to our own beliefs and attitudes.[55]

It has been remarked that when historians are asked for further explanation they go for more detail. Oakeshott said this in support of the anti-reductionist school of thought, but then he disputed the very notion of causation in history, believing that only a relation of events in a narrative could be offered as an historical explanation.[56] We should at least consider the opposite course of action, namely seeking further explanation of events through a generalisation. As with Cain and Hopkins, this does not mean abandoning careful research and detailed evidence initially. We are back to the issue of whether or not we want to make sense of the human experience through our collective history. What we have hoped to show in this section on historical explanation is that there are no easy answers to what constitutes the historical method of explanation. The relationship between narrative and analysis is a complex one, and though an awareness of philosophical distinctions on causation can help us to avoid confused debates, we should beware of critiques that try to impose a template of explanatory method. And, of course, in a supposedly postmodern world, explanation is not necessarily the objective. There has long been a distinction drawn between knowledge, often seen as scientific, and understanding which is seen as humanistic; but some postmodernists often want to go further along a continuum towards reporting experience without further 'understanding'.

Further reading

'Class' and Patrick Joyce

Joyce, P., *Democratic Subjects: The Self and the Social in Nineteenth Century England* (Cambridge University Press, 1991).

Joyce, P., (ed.), *Class* (Oxford University Press, 1995).

Kaye, H.J., *The British Marxist Historians* (Polity Press, 1984).

Thompson, E.P., 'Eighteenth-century English society: class struggle without class?', *Social History*, 3 (1978), pp. 146–50.

Class and the French Revolution

Cobban, A., *The Social Interpretation of the French Revolution* (Cambridge University Press, 1964).

Doyle, W., *Origins of the French Revolution* (Oxford University Press, 1980).

Furet, F., *Interpreting the French Revolution* (Cambridge University Press, 1981).

Gildea, R., *The Past in French History* (Yale University Press, 1994).

Lewis, G., *The French Revolution: Re-thinking the Debate* (Routledge, 1999).

Gentlemanly capitalists

Cain, P.J. and Hopkins, A.G., *British Imperialism, 1688–2000* (Longman, 2001).

Cannadine, D., *Ornamentalism: How the British Saw their Empire* (Allen Lane, 2001).

Said, E., *Orientalism* (Penguin, 2003).

Webster, A., *The Debate on the Rise of the British Empire* (Manchester University Press, 2006).

Notes

1 See especially F. Braudel, *The Mediterranean and the Mediterranean World in the Age of Philip II* (Fontana, 1975), first published in French in 1949; and Braudel, *Capitalism and Material Life* (Weidenfeld and Nicolson, 1973), first published in French in 1967; E. Le Roy Ladurie, *Montaillou: Cathars and Catholics in a French Village 1294–1324* (Penguin, 1980), first published in French in 1978.

2 A good appreciation of British Marxist historians is H.J. Kaye, *The British Marxist Historians* (Polity Press, 1984). A brief account of the Marxists' attempts to influence the profession is in C. Parker, *The English Historical Tradition since 1850* (John Donald, 1990), pp. 177–210.

3 R.G. Collingwood, *Speculum Mentis or the Map of Knowledge* (Clarendon Press, 1924), p. 237.

4 G.R. Elton, *The Practice of History* (Fontana, 1967); 'The historian's social function', *Transactions of the Royal Historical Society*, 5 (1977), pp. 197–211; Elton, *Return to Essentials: Some Reflections on the Present State of Historical Study* (Cambridge University Press, 1991), pp. 3–26.

5 E.P. Thompson, *The Making of the English Working Class* (Penguin, 1991), pp. 916–39.

6 Ibid, pp. 9–12; also E.P. Thompson, 'Eighteenth-century English society: class struggle without class?', *Social History*, 3 (1978), pp. 146–50.

7 Kaye, *The British Marxist Historians*, pp. 232–41.

8 P. Joyce, *Visions of the People: Industrial England and the Question of Class 1848–1914* (Cambridge University Press, 1991).

9 P. Joyce, *Democratic Subjects: The Self and the Social in Nineteenth-century England* (Cambridge University Press, 1994).

10 P. Joyce (ed.), *Class* (Oxford University Press, 1995), p. 3. Joyce had made the same points in *Democratic Subjects*, p. 2.

11 Joyce (ed.), *Class*, pp. 3–9.

12 Ibid., p. 14.

13 Joyce, *Democratic Subjects*, p. 1.

14 Ibid., p. 4.

15 Ibid., p. 22.

16 Ibid., p. 336.

17 C. Parker, *The English Idea of History from Coleridge to Collingwood* (Ashgate, 2000), p. 139.

18 A. Cobban, *The Social Interpretation of the French Revolution* (Cambridge University Press, 1964), p. 168. Though published in 1964, this was not the beginning of the Lefebvre–Cobban dispute (Lefebvre actually died in 1959). The 1964 book had originally been a lecture series in 1962; but Cobban's inaugural lecture in 1955 had attacked Lefebvre's position.

19 W. Doyle, *Origins of the French Revolution*, (Oxford University Press, 1980), p. 8.

20. Cobban, *The Social Interpretation of the French Revolution*, pp. 58–61.

21 Ibid., pp. 61–80.

22 We are indebted to Daniel Gordon for advice on French historiography, but we are responsible for the interpretation offered here.

23 F. Furet, *Interpreting the French Revolution* (Cambridge University Press/ Editions de le Maison des Sciences de l'Homme, 1981), p. 76.

24 Ibid., pp. 12, 18–22.

25 S. Schama, *Citizens: A Chronicle of the French Revolution* (Penguin Books, 1989), pp. xiv–xv.

26 R. Gildea, *The Past in French History* (Yale University Press, 1994) p. 2.

'Playful' is a term much appreciated by postmodernists.

27 Ibid., p. 10.

28 Ibid., p. 12.

29 K. Popper, *The Poverty of Historicism* (Routledge, 1994), p. 161.

30 See, for example, S. Berger, 'Viewpoint: Historians and nation-building in Germany after Reunification', *Past and Present*, 148 (1995), p. 188.

31 G.W.F. Hegel, *Hegel's Philosophy of Mind* (Clarendon Press, 1971), p. 277.

32 G.W.F. Hegel, *Lectures on the Philosophy of History* (Dale Publications, 1950).

33 H.A.L. Fisher, *A History of Europe*, vol. 1 (Eyre and Spottiswoode, 1943), p. vi.

34 R. Robinson and J. Gallagher, 'The imperialism of free trade', *Economic History Review* (2nd Series) i, 1953, pp. 1–15.

35 P. Cain and A. Hopkins, *British Imperialism: Innovation and Expansion Vol. 1, 1688–1914* (Longman, 1993) and *British Imperialism: Crisis and Deconstruction Vol. 2, 1914–1990* (Longman, 1993).

36 We are indebted to Tony Webster for his advice on Cain and Hopkins; his study of the historiography of imperialism in the Manchester University Press series on historiography should be referred to for a full consideration of the subject, A. Webster, *The Debate on the Rise of the British Empire*. As ever, any faults in our interpretation are our own and not his.

37 They answered their critics in a single-volume second edition of *British Imperialism* eight years later: P.J. Cain and A.G. Hopkins, *British Imperialism, 1688–2000* (2nd edn, Longman, 2001), pp. 1–19.

38 Cain and Hopkins, *British Imperialism*, 2nd edn, pp. 2–4, 6–7, 12–13.

39 D. Cannadine, *Ornamentalism: How the British Saw their Empire* (Allen Lane, 2001), pp. xvi–xvii.

40 Ibid., pp. xiii, xx, 121, 136–49, 174–9.

41 Ibid., pp. xxii, 181–99.

42 Ibid., pp. 41, 58–9, 71.

43 Ibid., pp. 153–73.

44 E. Said, *Orientalism* (Penguin, 2003), p. 334. Also see p. 342.

45 F. Fukuyama, *The End of History and the Last Man* (Free Press, 1992).

46 Samuel P. Huntington, *The Clash of Civilizations and the Remaking of World Order* (Touchstone Books, 1998).

47 For example, Jared Diamond, *Collapse: how societies choose to fail or survive* (Allen Lane, 2005).

48 Quoted by Peter Munz in P. Munz, 'The historical narrative', in M. Bentley, *Companion to Historiography* (Routledge, 1998) p. 860.

49 I. Kershaw, *Hitler 1889–1936: Hubris* (Allen Lane, 1999); *Hitler 1936–1945: Nemesis* (Allen Lane, 2000).

50 Joyce, *Democratic Subjects*, pp. 154, 156.
51 Oakeshott, *Experience and Its Modes*, pp. 89, 92–3, 95.
52 Parker, *The English Idea of History from Coleridge to Collingwood*, p. 37.
53 Quentin Tarantino's film, *Pulp Fiction* for example, abandons the conventional narrative.
54 E.H. Carr, *What is History?* (Macmillan, 1961), p. 99.
55 Parker, *The English Idea of History from Coleridge to Collingwood*, p. 112.
56 Oakeshott, *Experience and Its Modes*, pp. 142–4.

4

The essay and historiography

Introduction

Despite the development of a variety of forms of assessment – textual analyses, book reviews, article summaries and statistical analyses, to name a few – the written essay still retains a central role on many undergraduate history degree programmes. There are many good reasons for this. The ability to construct a clear coherent case, supported by argument, evidence and references is an obviously valuable skill, as is recognised in the subject benchmarking statement for History, drawn up by the Quality Assurance Agency (QAA).[1] However, while there is a great deal of material that deals with the process of writing an essay, in particular focusing on issues of planning and structuring, there is relatively little that considers the fundamental nature of the essay, and how it relates to the broader historiographical issues dealt with elsewhere in this book.[2] The first part of this chapter will consider that specific issue, and the second will then examine the wider benefits of developing an aptitude for writing essays.

The nature of the essay

When students are asked to account for the outbreak of revolution in France in 1789, what is expected of them? At first glance the response to this seems obvious; they have to explain the reasons for the French Revolution. This, though, raises the question: how will they do that? They will not, unless they are very remarkable students with plenty of time and money visit French archives and begin wading through the documents of the late eighteenth century. No, good students will get themselves to their libraries and assemble a pile of books dealing with the subject. Having assembled enough books it might be thought, and some students undoubtedly do think this, that the next task is to sit down and extract a reasonable number of causes of the French Revolution, paraphrase them, reproduce them and submit the work. Anybody approaching an essay in this fashion can expect at best a lower second-class mark, in percentage terms between 50 and 60 per cent.

There are at least three reasons why the approach outlined above is inadequate: firstly, it demonstrates a very low level skill; whatever else degree-level history is about, it is not about rewarding your ability to paraphrase other people's works. Secondly this approach usually ignores vital distinctions between the types of book on library shelves. Broadly speaking these are either textbooks or monographs.[3] (For a much fuller discussion of genres of historical writing, see Chapter 2). Textbooks usually aim to provide information about a broad sweep of historical development. David Childs's *Britain Since 1939*, for example 'is about the general developments in British politics' from 1939 to the 1990s.[4] Works of this nature inevitably condense the subject matter that they deal with. Monographs are much more specialised works that deal with shorter time spans, explicitly argue for a particular interpretation, and are often, but not always based upon the author's Ph.D. thesis. James Hinton's *The First Shop Stewards' Movement* meets all of these criteria.[5] It deals with a particular trade union development in one industry – engineering – over a 10-year period, and takes 343 pages to do this. In comparison Childs covers the entire political history of Britain over a 60-year period in 294 pages. It might be thought that the purpose of this comparison is to suggest that monographs are more useful simply because they are more detailed. This response would, though, miss the point at issue. History students do need to know the details of particular events and developments, and textbooks can play a crucial role in giving them that knowledge. However, and here we move on to our third objection, historical scholarship is rarely about discovering the specific details of an event or development. It is more usually concerned with the significance of those details. In Chapter 3 it was stated that the late E.P. Thompson believed that it was a fact that the English working class created itself between 1780 and 1830. This view is hotly disputed by some historians to this day. However, the information that Thompson cited to support his case is largely undisputed. What is at issue, then, are not the details of the period, but the interpretation that Thompson developed from them.

The process of deciding the significance of particular events, inevitably, as E.H. Carr pointed out, involves a process of selection.[6] Factors that are seen as relatively unimportant may be downplayed or even ignored completely by the author of a monograph. Consequently, to return to the assignment on the French Revolution, the student who simply reproduces the causes given in a monograph will reproduce the author's selection of causes, without offering any rationale for the selection. Such an approach will at best produce a limited treatment of the subject, and at worst, produce a piece of work that is seriously one-sided. Where is this leading, you might be asking at this juncture? The answer is embedded in three key points: firstly that it is not possible (or, indeed, appropriate) for History undergraduates to conduct primary research for their essay assignments, that is, apart from dissertations and extended essays usually undertaken in the final year of degree programmes. Secondly, that the mere extraction of causes/factors from either textbooks or monographs is an unsatisfactory approach. Thirdly, that academic history is primarily concerned with explaining and interpreting events and developments, not simply describing them. Taken together what this adds up to is that most undergraduate history assignments require students to assess the validity of existing published interpretations. In the case of this particular question students would have to discuss, if they wished to achieve marks at or above the 2.1 level, the interpretations advanced by Lefebvre and Cobban (see Chapter 3) and by subsequent contributors to the debate, such as François Furet and Tim Blanning.[7]

Generally speaking then the undergraduate history essay is an exercise in the assessment of existing historical interpretations. A number of points follow on from this. Students should, when considering an assignment question, attempt to identify the debate to which it relates. Nearly all assignment questions either directly, or indirectly, refer to such debates. Take the following question, for example: To what degree was the Soviet Union responsible for the onset of the first Cold War? Although it does not explicitly mention it, this question relates to the changes in the interpretation of the Cold War that have taken place since 1945. In the immediate post-Second World War period, interpretations, like those of Herbert Feis, *From Trust to Terror: The Onset of the Cold War, 1945– 50*, tended to stress the aggressive expansionist nature of Soviet Marxism. In the 1960s, possibly influenced by the experience of the Vietnam War, which led many Americans to critically reflect on their own nation's policies and history, a 'revisionist' school of Cold War historians emerged. Figures like David Horowitz, *From Yalta to Vietnam* (a significant title) tended to stress the defensive nature of Soviet foreign policy, and the aggressive character of US policy; a clear reversal of roles. In more recent times a new school of 'post-revisionists' have come to the fore. Historians like J.L. Gaddis, *The United States and the Origins of the Cold War 1941– 47*, occupy a halfway position, characterising the United States's moves to expand its influence as essentially defensive, designed to contain the Soviet Union and maintain a balance of world power.[8] What appears to be a relatively straightforward question is, therefore, underpinned by a considerable body of scholarship.

Having identified the parameters of the debate, students are faced with two tasks. The first is to make sure that they have a sufficiently detailed knowledge of the events and developments to understand their full significance. This can usually be acquired relatively painlessly by the use of textbooks. The next task is to select an appropriate number of the most prominent protagonists in the debate, the critical assessment of whose interpretations will then form the basis of the essay.

Approaches to the essay

A crucial starting point when approaching an essay question is, then, to identify the historical debate to which it directly or indirectly refers. For example, having thus recognised that the question: 'Mass unemployment or mass consumerism: which best characterises life in Britain in the 1930s?' refers to the debate between 'pessimistic' and 'optimistic' interpretations of that decade, the nature of the task posed becomes clear.[9] The essay requires a critical evaluation of each position. The key to this process of evaluation lies in the nature of historical scholarship as it has developed since the nineteenth century (see Chapter 2). Historians do not make up their accounts; their claims and interpretations have to be supported by primary evidence, secondary scholarship, argumentation, or a combination of two or more of these elements. The evaluation of a historical interpretation will, therefore, involve a critical examination of the role played by these elements.

Primary evidence is generally seen as evidence that was created in the period under discussion, for example, a charter, or a royal statute. Some students have a tendency to see such material as innately superior to other forms of evidence, simply by dint of its provenance. However, it should always be remembered that primary materials are themselves often intrinsically biased, to the extent that they are shaped by the agendas of their authors. William Booth, the founder of the Salvation Army provided a vivid account of life in the slum districts of late nineteenth-century England in his *Darkest England and the Way Out*, but it is an account based on the premise that the people of such areas primarily needed to be saved, like the natives of 'Darkest Africa', by the actions of Christian missionaries.[10] It is also a mistake to believe that primary materials allow students to access the past in its entirety. E.H. Carr joked that medieval historians were fortunate that so little evidence survived from their period, as it made it easier to deal with.[11] However, the problem of incomplete records also affects some much more recent periods. The historians of twentieth-century British television, for example, are seriously handicapped by the fact that production companies in the 1950s and 1960s did not keep copies of much of their programme output. As a consequence, even the complete body of surviving evidence for particular topics may only give an incomplete and partial view. Despite these observations, primary sources remain the essential materials with which

the historian has to work. Even those historians who regard themselves as postmodernists, and argue that all human experience exists only in the form of language embodied in texts, still focus
upon texts that are recognised (presumably 'within language') as
being of the past.[12] The task for the undergraduate is to decide
whether the use made of such material is both legitimate and convincing.

Historians use primary sources in a great many ways. In the first
example to be considered, John Baxendale and Christopher Pawling
use a lengthy quotation to convey what they argue were the political views of the writer, J.B. Priestley, in the Second World War.
The quote is used to support their contention that during the
Second World War, the political left – broadly defined – developed a form of polemic that incorporated a negative view of Britain
in the interwar period. The purpose of this polemic was to promote the idea that the war was not simply about defeating the
Germans, but was also about creating a radically different society
after the war. This they called the 'People's War' narrative. Counterposed to this was the 'Churchillian' narrative, which utilised traditional, often rural and heroic images from the more distant past,
and was linked to a conservative view of the war's objectives.[13] The
quotation used is as follows:

> Surely one reason why the last twenty years now seem a tragic farce,
> even here at home, is that during this period we did not change values
> but merely cheapened them. It will be remembered as the era of night-
> club haunting princes and gossip-writing peers. The masquerade still
> went on, though now the costumes were tattered and the masks rot-
> ting ... no visitor to Britain seeing the ruined cotton mills and rotting
> shipyards of the North, the jerry-built bungalows and gimcrack facto-
> ries of the South, exclaimed in wonder as men had done once, at the
> virility, splendour and potent magic of our island life. How much was
> there here worth preserving ... The nation's mind was elsewhere, with-
> drawn, more than half asleep, charmed and lulled by politicians with
> a good bedside manner.[14]

On the face of it this quotation supports Baxendale and Pawling's
argument. The political points that Priestley made in 1941 were
clearly underpinned by a negative interpretation of the inter-war

years. Like many historians, Baxendale and Pawling have edited their quotation to emphasise the elements that support their position. However, the curious – and historians should always be curious – might wonder what has been left out. Between the words 'rotting' and 'no visitor' the original contained the following lines:

> Meanwhile the last traces were vanishing of that older Britain whose hazy loveliness was recorded by Turner and Constable, Girtin and Cotman, whose wealth of character enriched the pages of Fielding and Sterne, Scott and Dickens, whose love and pain and ecstasy were made immortal by her lyric poets. Among these vanishing traces, which gave a special savour to this island, were quaint customs and quirks of local thought and feeling, quiet forgotten corners and immemorial traditions. It was nothing of this that the Conservatives succeeded in conserving, but only the secret of how to make money and retain power. This older Britain had to go, but what took its place had no like value, no new salt and savour; and no visitor to Britain seeing ...[15]

This extract is very different in nature, in that it refers to a more distant past and expresses regret for lost features of pre-industrial Britain. In other words it seems to be, to use Baxendale and Pawling's term, 'Churchillian' in character. These lines do not, of themselves, call into question Baxendale and Pawling's interpretation, which is based on much more than one quotation, but they at least suggest that the evidence can be read in other ways, and that maybe the distinction between the 'People's War' and 'Churchillian' narratives is not as strong as they suggest.

Students may object that they do not have time to access the original primary materials that would enable them to make such points. Historians, though, are an argumentative lot, and often go into print to take issue with their colleagues. Consequently, the diligent student will often be able to find such material in published form in journals, reviews and even in works that are written as acts of rebuttal.[16] Contentious works, like A.J.P. Taylor's *The Origins of the Second World War* often provoke a considerable body of work, written in response.[17] This provides excellent material for student essay writers. Daniel Jonah Goldhagen's *Hitler's Willing Executioners: Ordinary Germans and the Holocaust* is a similarly contentious book, and has also provoked a considerable number of responses. Goldhagen argues that anti-Semitism was a deep-seated feature of German culture, and had been long before Hitler came to power. The significance of this cultural attribute was that, as expressed in his title, 'ordinary Germans' were the 'willing executioners' of the Jewish people.[18] Norman Finkelstein points out that a large element of the evidence used by Goldhagen to support these contentions comes from the 'self-incriminating testimony of the police battalions' (units directly involved in the mass killings of Jews). Moreover, Finkelstein argues that Goldhagen uses this material in a highly selective fashion. Accounts which demonstrate the savagery and brutality of the Germans' actions are cited in support of his interpretation; whereas any attempt by any of the witnesses to lessen their responsibility by, for example, saying that they were threatened by a superior officer, is dismissed out of hand.[19] This example on its own does not undermine Goldhagen's interpretation, but 'his blanket dismissal of all testimony impeaching his thesis' does, in this instance, raise a question about the legitimacy of Goldhagen's use of evidence.[20] Goldhagen's justification for this approach to this particular body of evidence rests on its equivocal nature, as the testimony of perpetrators collected by the West German authorities after the war. Clearly, it would seem that many such individuals would be likely to attempt to put the best possible construction on their actions in order to lessen the consequences. Even Goldhagen recognised that: 'some truthful self-exonerations will be dismissed because of this methodological position'. He goes on however to state that his work supports the belief that 'such uncorroborated true statements are few'.[21] It is not our purpose here to attempt to establish the validity of either side of the argument, but rather to demonstrate how such issues form the basis of historical debates, and provide points of entry for those writing undergraduate essays.

As has been said before, historians use primary sources in a variety of ways, and it is not possible to consider them all here. The key point that students have to ask is: does the use of the evidence really support the interpretation being presented? The eminent historian of Nazi Germany, Ian Kershaw has stated, and most historians would agree with him, that, 'debate and controversy are the very essence of historical study'.[22] This means that every historical interpretation that ever emerges is scrutinised and sometimes criticised by other historians. This process acts, among other things, as a form of quality control, more or less successfully ensuring that historians conform to certain standards of scholarship. At the same time this discussion generates a body of literature that provides an easy access to the debates of academic historians for the undergraduate history student. It also indicates how historical knowledge grows. This is not usually the result of startling discoveries of new evidence, but is rather more like a geological accumulation of understanding, as successive historians take the interpretations of the subject in new directions via a combination of new knowledge and insights. This means that each new interpretation stands in a relationship to a multitude of pre-existing interpretations. Thus, when John Stevenson and Chris Cook argued in 1979 that most people were better off in 1939 than they had been ten years earlier, they were presenting a challenge to the emphasis of many pre-existing views, such as those of Branson and Heinemann, who had argued that all Britain's rulers had been able to achieve in the 1930s was: 'a partial and precarious economic recovery'.[23]

The interlocking nature of historical knowledge thus points to another approach to assessing a historical interpretation: how does it relate to other works written about the same subject? This relationship usually takes two forms. Firstly, a book is written to promote a new interpretation and often in the process directly challenges an existing interpretation; this is clearly the case with Stevenson and Cook's *The Slump: Society and Politics During the Depression*, which questioned the validity of the 'pessimistic' view of Britain in the 1930s. In the process of calling into question works like Branson and Heinemann's *Britain in the Nineteen Thirties*, Cook and Stevenson also cite previously published works which support their views.[24]

The direct clash of interpretation is, we have already suggested, the central element of any essay, but the secondary works cited in support by the protagonists provide a point at which the validity of their claims can be assessed. Goldhagen's work again offers a number of examples here. Finkelstein notes that he cites the work of Ian Kershaw to demonstrate that Hitler was a genuinely popular figure in Nazi Germany. Finkelstein suggests that this is not a legitimate use of Kershaw's work because Goldhagen does not acknowledge that this author rejects the idea of anti-Semitism playing a central role in the relationship between the Führer and the German people.[25] This raises some interesting issues because Goldhagen cites Kershaw to demonstrate Hitler's popularity, but not to prove that Hitler was popular because of his anti-Semitism.[26] Goldhagen clearly believes that Hitler's popularity was essentially the product of anti-Semitism, but that is not the point that is being made where Kershaw is cited. The legitimacy of the citation is arguable, demonstrating that analysing the use of secondary sources is not always straightforward. It raises the question: does a citation involve the invocation of the entire argument of a specific book, or of a specific point within it? The answer is that that both kinds of citation can occur, and the historian, or undergraduate, has to use their judgement to decide which is being used in any particular case.

In the above example, Finkelstein questions Goldhagen's use of another secondary source to support his case. Another issue that often emerges is where historians are accused of failing to cite the appropriate publications. By doing so, they fail to locate their work within the existing matrix of historical interpretation. This type of charge is often to be found in book reviews. In his 2003 review of Peter Mandler's *History and National Life*, Professor Arthur Marwick expressed this type of criticism, with characteristic vigour:

> Mandler dismisses all others who have written on the uses of history, who, he says, without giving any names or examples, 'tend to lump together incompatible goals or to collapse into incoherent generalisations.[27]

Marwick obviously feels that Mandler is guilty of a lapse of scholarship in failing to properly cite those unnamed authors. The validity of his claim need not detain us, what is important to remember is that failing to cite is as important a point of criticism, as citing inaccurately. In passing, it is worth noting that book reviews, particularly in historical journals, can be invaluable to history students as they provide, at their best, condensed introductions to the historiographical issues surrounding particular topics. *Reviews in History,* an electronic journal maintained by the Institute of Historical Research is an especially useful resource as it enables the original authors to respond to their reviewers; this provides an illuminating insight into the processes of historical debate.[28]

Historians do not simply allow historical sources to 'speak for themselves'. Information from sources is elected, shaped and linked to published, secondary material to build an argument; meaning in this context, a case. The next issue that has to be addressed is that of argumentation. Here the student has to test the coherence, logic and integrity of the interpretation under examination. In other words the student has to critically consider the way that the historian has used his or her sources and references. As always this can be best illustrated by use of examples.

In the authorised biography of the Labour politician, Barbara Castle, Anne Perkins claimed that the Labour party's defeat in the 1951 General Election was in large part the consequence of internal party divisions between the left- and right-wings.[29] In this Perkins was following both the 'common-sense' of British politics, and the Labour Party's own view of its history.[30] It is true that the party was divided, and it is also true that the party lost the 1951 election, however, the link between these two developments is not as obvious as it at first appears. Firstly, the Labour party won nearly 14 million votes, more than the Conservatives, and indeed the largest vote 'ever won by any British political party'.[31] The problem was not the internal divisions of the Labour party, but the financial difficulties of the Liberals, which meant that the party fielded a smaller number of candidates and there were fewer three-cornered contests, a situation which enabled the Conservatives to win the election, even though they gained a smaller share of the total vote. Kenneth O. Morgan consequently concludes: 'The Bevanite [the left-wing faction] divisions evidently had little, if any effect.'[32] Both writers had equal access to the same information, indeed, Perkins noted the size of Labour's 1951 vote, but both chose to place a different interpretation on that information. In a situation of this kind a student would have to decide which, in terms of the deployment of information and the application of logic, is the most convincing.

The example given above, of the impact of the Bevanites in the Labour party, deals with different interpretations being placed upon evidence; sometimes though, historians use literary devices to convey a sense of their analysis. E.P. Thompson, for example, placed a great deal of emphasis upon the idea of the cultural transmission of a long-term tradition of British radicalism.[33] In *The Making of the English Working Class* he argued that the radical tradition was transmitted and embodied within religious non-conformity; more specifically, he claimed that radicals of the late eighteenth century were informed in their views by the traditions of the seventeenth century: 'No one with Bunyan in their bones could have found many of Blake's aphorisms strange'.[34] This quotation does, though, highlight one of the problems with Thompson's view of the transmission of tradition: how does it take place? One solution is to see the tradition as being embodied in individuals, like the Quaker-educated Tom Paine, author of *Rights of Man* (1790), a tract in support of the French Revolution. However, Paine, born in 1737, was at some historical distance from the radicals of the English Civil War, and indeed did not show any signs of radicalism until the 1770s. His radicalism could therefore be seen as much as the product of contextual circumstances, as of the operation of a long-term tradition. Thompson also uses literary devices to convey his sense of the operation of this tradition.

> The intellectual history of Dissent is made up of collisions, schisms, mutations; and one feels often that the dormant seeds of political Radicalism lie within it, ready to germinate whenever planted in a benevolent and hopeful social context.[35]

This clearly works as a literary metaphor, drawing on the language of biology, but does it work as a historical argument? The answer must be no, because it does not rest on evidence but on a striking image relating to processes that do not apply to human beings, presumably the repositories of these 'seeds' of radicalism. As with the other examples given, this does not discredit Thompson's arguments; it is cited, rather, as an example of a specific kind of historical argument that students may well encounter. It is also fair to say, though, that the idea of the unconscious transmission of traditions does occur in other places in Thompson's writings. In his essay, 'Peculiarities of the English', for example, he claims:

> I have often noted the glassy look coming over a working-class audience when being addressed by a strident advocate of this or that brand of orthodox Marxism, as if the tone, far more than the argument, stirred in the collective unconscious some memory of the apparitor, the summoner and the arch-deacon's courts.[36]

The idea that Marxist zealots are seen in the same light as the purveyors of past orthodoxies is an attractive one, but the claim, which is made in a polemic about historical traditions, does raise the troubling question of how Thompson might demonstrate, using historically acceptable evidence, the existence of such a 'collective unconscious'.

Plagiarism

One of the key points that this book intends to put over, is that history is an evidence-based subject. From this follows the subject's stress on the importance of the apparently humble, but in reality crucial, footnote or endnote (see Chapter 2). From this also follows what has been discussed earlier in this chapter, that is to critically analyse an historical interpretation involves examining the range and nature of sources utilised, and also the way in which the sources are shaped and edited to construct a historical argument. By and large, historians produce original historical interpretations and history students learn, as an essential part of their training, in the writing of essays, how to test the coherence and validity of those interpretations. If students keep these points in the forefront of their minds, then they should avoid the ultimate transgression, for historians, of plagiarism. Before explaining why this is the case we need to explain what plagiarism is.

Plagiarism occurs when a student, or, indeed, anyone else, passes off somebody else's work as their own. Some students do consciously and maliciously plagiarise. It is ultimately a self-defeating exercise because, although such a student may be awarded a degree, we emphasise 'may', as most such individuals are caught, they will not have acquired the skills and aptitudes that the degree is supposed to indicate. Crudely, it is the equivalent of having a driving licence without being able to drive. However, many other students fall into plagiarism because they do not understand the nature of the enterprise. If, to go back to our earlier example, students believe that they have to provide a direct answer to the question of why a revolution occurred in late eighteenth-century France, they are likely do so by culling and paraphrasing causes from published secondary works. In such a process it is easy to cross the line from paraphrasing to reproducing material directly from the book being used. The reason why it is easy to cross that line is because methodologically paraphrasing material is very similar to copying; in both cases information is being reproduced from another person's work. If, on the other hand the student is clear that the essay requires an examination and critique of a number of interpretations, then this unconscious plagiarism is unlikely to occur, because the student will be following a different process. The student who attempts to answer the question will simply be saying: these are the causes, all culled from other authors. The student who focuses on interpretations will be saying: these are some of the explanations that historians have come up with, and these are their strengths and weaknesses, as I see them. This is a much more complex process, and it is one that consciously acknowledges that the explanations being examined derive from the work of published historians.

Writing conclusions

As students move towards the conclusion of their essays they have to decide which of the interpretations, or combination of interpretations, is most convincing. At this point it is tempting to state in a clear straightforward manner: 'I think' etc. Historians generally avoid the use of the first person 'I'. The reason for this is that they are generally talking about events and developments of which they have no first-hand experience. Using the first person implies a degree of direct knowledge that is inappropriately subjective, as is explained in Chapter 3. It is perhaps worth noting that historians influenced by postmodernism do, on occasion, use the first person. The rationale for this is the belief that the past as separate entity does not exist, and that history is a narrative created in a permanent present, that only comes into being when the historian produces it. In this perspective then, there is no separation between the objective past and the subjective historian, consequently in the view of such writers, the use of the first person is perfectly acceptable.[37] It is important to note this view, if only because it demonstrates that within history it is not simply the interpretation of events in the past that are contested; increasingly it is the very nature of the subject that is called into question. Having said that, it seems reasonable to say that most historians in practice agree with Lawrence Stone, that History is about gaining knowledge of a past, which was, although by definition gone, a separate entity from the present.[38] Consequently, for most working historians the point about the use of the first person remains true.

Another issue confronting students considering the conclusion of their essays is that of support; given that they usually depend on secondary sources it is vital that every statement is supported, either by references and/or argumentation. If, for example, one were discussing the response of Labour's left-wing to the German-Soviet Non-Aggression Pact of 1939, it would be perfectly valid to argue that, given his known political opinions, it would be extremely unlikely that the left-wing MP, Aneurin Bevan, had no views on the treaty. It would also be valid to go on to argue that the fact that Bevan's biographer and political comrade, Michael Foot, gives the Pact only the briefest mention, and says nothing about Bevan's view of it, seems almost like an act of concealment by omission.[39] The process here is one where an extrapolation is made from two known details; Bevan's sympathy for the Soviet Union, and the impact of the German-Soviet Pact upon British left-wingers, to make a supported inference.[40] Further support can be added by referring to secondary works; for example an article published in *Socialist History* in 1996 quoted from a euphorically supportive account of the German-Soviet Pact published in 1940, by Michael

Foot.[41] In a similar, but briefer vein, Barbara Castle's authorised biographer also includes a claim that Bevan supported the Pact.[42] This combination of argumentation and secondary material enables us to say three things about this issue: firstly, that it was unlikely that members of the British left would have no views on this treaty; secondly, that leading figures on the left supported the Pact; and, finally, that subsequently the leading figures of the left appeared reluctant to discuss the Pact. To move further than this, for example to make comments on why they were so reluctant to discuss it, without further support in the form of argumentation, would be to move into the realms of unhistorical speculation and assertion.

Quotations can also be used to support an argument, but they should be used sparingly in an undergraduate essay of around 2,000 words. The purpose of such an essay is to demonstrate that you, the student, can critically engage with historical interpretations; lengthy quotations use up valuable space, which could be better used developing the argument. The overuse of, particularly long, quotations may well be taken as demonstrating your ignorance, rather than your erudition; it will look as if you are trying to address the question in someone else's words, because you are unable to do it directly.

Historians are full of woes; depending on the subject, they will lament the lack of evidence, and they will lament its over-abundance. No historian will nowadays claim, as Lord Acton once did, that there will ever be a completion of history.[43] This is both because of the problems posed by the quantity of evidence, and also the fact that interpretations change over time, as the perspective of historians changes. What this means is that the conclusions drawn by historians are always provisional, rather than fixed for all time. Some historians respond to this situation by producing very general, non-contentious conclusions. Andrew Thorpe ends his book *A History of the British Labour Party*, by stating that the party will face challenges in the future, produced by a range of political changes and developments.[44] As nothing, let alone the political situation, ever stays still, and as political parties always face challenges of one sort or another, these seem like fairly safe conclusions to draw. Those historians who take a more forthright approach to their conclusions often find themselves mocked by subsequent developments. In 1972 Ralph Miliband argued that the Labour Party was kept alive by the belief of many of its members that it would at some point transform itself into a true socialist party. From this followed his call for such people to abandon this illusion, and help create a true, socialist alternative.[45] After 1997 we have seen a Labour Party that has enthusiastically abandoned the last vestiges of socialism, achieve more political successes than at any previous stage in its existence. Miliband's view that the party was sustained by the illusory beliefs of its left-wing socialist members was shipwrecked by the changing tides of history. The point is that all historical conclusions, whether written by professional academics or by undergraduates, are necessarily provisional in nature. Consequently, it is wise to qualify one's statements, particularly one's concluding statements. What this means is not baldly saying that such a thing is so, but rather saying that the evidence would seem to suggest that it is so. It may sound trivial, but qualified statements recognise that one key element of the subject is its lack of fixity; what may seem beyond question in the present may well be considered in radically different terms, in a year or two.

History and the wider world

In a memorable passage, the American historian Deborah Lipstadt likened historians to the canaries that were used in nineteenth-century mines to detect poisonous gases.[46] In doing so Lipstadt, who was discussing the pernicious work of Holocaust-deniers, was arguing that historians have a special role to play in exposing questionable uses of history in public debate. This is a very important point that can be broadened to include all public debate, which frequently uses appeals to historical precedents and antecedents. The knowledge gained by history students and the skills and aptitudes that they develop as they learn to write historically have a significance that extends well beyond the seminar room; they can, and should, play a vital role in the functioning of the democratic process. As always, this can best be illustrated by the use of examples.

In the run-up to the invasion of Iraq, politicians and commentators on both sides of the Atlantic drew parallels between Saddam Hussein and Adolf Hitler. Donald Rumsfeld, the American Secretary of Defence, used such a parallel to deal with the question of whether there was sufficient evidence to prove the existence of weapons of mass destruction.

> Think of all the countries that said, well, we don't have enough evidence. I mean *Mein Kampf* had been written. Hitler had indicated what he wanted to do. Maybe he won't attack us. Maybe you won't do this or that. Well, there were millions of people dead because of this miscalculation.[47]

History students should, as they progress through their degrees, become aware that historical debates are related to the contexts within which they are produced. Similarly, public debates and interventions take shape within contexts. In the case of the Rumsfeld extract, part of the context was the desire of the American government to make legitimate the idea of attacking Iraq. Another contextual element was the fact that many people in the West had a negative perception of Hitler's role in history. Consequently, the objective of the Hitler–Saddam parallel was to promote the idea that the Iraqi leader had to be dealt with militarily, as had been the case with Hitler in the Second World War.

The second approach the historian might take to this extract is to examine the internal strength of the argument. What Rumsfeld wanted his audience to take away from his statement was the idea that if Saddam was not dealt with quickly, the West would face a level of devastation similar to that which resulted from the Second World War. What Rumsfeld actually said, though, was that the politicians of the 1930s did not act when they *had* evidence: *Mein Kampf*. Logically, this did not support the idea of going to war without conclusive evidence, which was what Rumsfeld wanted.[48] This was not, of course, a logical argument, but an associational one. The Secretary of State was concerned primarily to sell the war by making Saddam the new Hitler.

A final approach that a historian might make to this extract would be to ask: what is the evidence to support it? The very first point one might make is that now a considerable body of historians reject the notion that *Mein Kampf* laid out in advance the policies that Hitler followed, once in power (see Chapter 6).[49] That aside, it will also be useful to conduct a simple comparison of the policies and experiences of the two leaders. Hitler's foreign policy between 1933 and the outbreak of war involved a series of territorial expansions and infringements of the Treaty of Versailles, beginning with the re-militarisation of the Rhineland and ending with the occupation of Czechoslovakia in 1939. During that period the western powers took no effective action against him. Iraq invaded Kuwait in August 1990. Saddam's forces were forced out of Kuwait with considerable losses early in 1991. Subsequently, the Iraqis did not appear to threaten any further invasions. This suggests that the parallel between the two leaders is, at the very least, questionable. It also – taken together with the points about context, and the internal logic of the argument – demonstrates that the approaches developed by historians enable them to engage critically and actively in public debates of this nature.

This point can be further illustrated by looking at the role of historians in a society that restricted public debate. Nikita Khrushchev, head of the Soviet state from 1953 to 1964, declared: 'Historians are dangerous people. They are capable of upsetting everything'.[50] In Khrushchev's Soviet Union meaningful public debate did not take place; instead, one official view on all issues predominated. One official view of the present required an official view of the past to underpin it. The enquiries of historians could, potentially, threaten that structure, therefore they had to be constrained. Or, as one Soviet historian put it in 1961:

> Where the history of the Party is concerned, we have to think of the immediate needs of education; we can't always pursue purely academic objectives. Things have to be presented in a certain way; there are *more* important things than the purely objective enumeration of the facts.[51]

This runs entirely counter to the approaches to history that we have been talking about, because the end result of the historians' analyses were decided *before* they started working. If the Party had decided that Trotsky was a counter-revolutionary enemy of the people, then that became written into the historical record.

Summary

It probably seems a long way to move, from the writing of undergraduate history essays, to the curtailment of academic freedom in authoritarian regimes, so it might be useful to sum up how we moved from one to the other.

Academic history is structured around debates about interpretations of events and developments. Undergraduates access history principally through secondary works (the writings of professional historians). This means that essay questions should be approached as assessments of interpretations. To conduct such assessments students have to: identify the debate their question addresses; select an appropriate variety of conflicting interpretations; assess the value of those interpretations, taking into account their use of primary and secondary evidence and the coherence of their argument; and finally present a supported conclusion about the interpretations under discussion. In the process of developing and refining this approach, students will develop many useful analytical, research, communication and case-building skills, which can be transferred to a range of careers. They will also develop a range of critical aptitudes that will make them better able to act as full citizens in democratic societies.

Further reading

M. Abbott (ed.), *History Skills* (Routledge, 1996).
J. Black and D.M. MacRaild, *Studying History* (Palgrave, 2000).
E.H. Carr, *What is History?* (Palgrave, 2001).
G.R. Elton, *The Practice of History* (Blackwell, 2001).
A. Marwick, *The New Nature of History* (Palgrave, 2001).
J. Tosh, *The Pursuit of History* (Longman, 2005).

Notes

1 Quality Assurance Agency for Higher Education, *Subject Benchmarking Statement for History* (QAA, 2000), available at www.qaa.ac.uk.
2 See, for example, M. Abbott (ed.), *History Skills* (Routledge, 1996).
3 This categorisation is something of a simplification for the purposes of our argument. For a much fuller categorisation of history books, see A. Marwick, *The New Nature of History* (Palgrave, 2001), pp. 228–30.

4 D. Childs, *Britain Since 1939: Progress and Decline* (Macmillan, 1995), p. xiii.

5 J. Hinton, *The First Shop Stewards' Movement* (George Allen and Unwin, 1973).

6 E.H. Carr, *What is History?* (Palgrave, 2001), p. 18.

7 For an outline of more recent developments in the debate around the French Revolution see G. Lewis, *The French Revolution: Re-thinking the Debate* (Routledge, 1999).

8 For an outline of these debates see: K. Larres and A. Lane, *The Cold War* (Blackwell, 2001).

9 For a pessimistic account see N. Branson and M. Heinemann, *Britain in the Nineteen Thirties* (Weidenfeld and Nicolson, 1971). For an optimistic account see C. Cook, *Britain in the Depression: Society and Politics 1929–1939* (Longman, 1994).

10 W. Booth, *Darkest England and the Way Out* (Salvation Army, 1890).

11 Carr, *What is History?*, p. 8.

12 See, for example, P. Joyce's use of the nineteenth-century diary of Edwin Waugh, in *Democratic Subjects: The Self and the Social in Nineteenth Century England* (Cambridge University Press, 1994), p. 23.

13 J. Baxendale and C. Pawling, *Narrating the Thirties: A Decade in the Making 1930 to the Present* (Macmillan, 1996) p. 2.

14 Ibid., pp. 135–6.

15 J.B. Priestley, *Out of the People* (William Heinemann Ltd., 1941), pp. 105–6.

16 A discussion of Baxendale and Pawling's work is contained in, for example, R. Spalding, 'Popular Historiography and the Second World War', *Socialist History*, Spring 1999, pp. 54–67.

17 A.J.P. Taylor, *The Origins of the Second World War* (Penguin, 1964); E.M. Robinson (ed.), *The Origins of the Second World War* (Macmillan, 1976); G. Martel (ed.), *The Origins of the Second World War Reconsidered: A.J.P. Taylor and the Historians* (Routledge, 1999).

18 D.J. Goldhagen, *Hitler's Willing Executioners* (Little, Brown and Company, 1996), p. 9.

19 N.G. Finkelstein and R.B. Birn, *A Nation On Trial: The Goldhagen Thesis and Historical Truth* (Henry Holt & Co., 1998), pp. 71–2.

20 Ibid., p. 71.

21 Goldhagen, *Hitler's Willing Executioners* (Little, Brown & Co., 1996), p. 601.

22 I. Kershaw, *The Nazi Dictatorship: Problems and Perspectives of Interpretation* (Edward Arnold, 1993), p. 1.

23 J. Stevenson and C. Cook, *The Slump: Society and Politics During the Depression*

(Quartet, 1979), p. 5; Branson and Heinemann, *Britain in the Nineteen Thirties* (Panther, 1971), p. 18.

24 Stevenson and Cook, *The Slump*, p. 325.

25 Finkelstein and Birn, *A Nation On Trial*, pp. 31–2.

26 Goldhagen, *Hitler's Willing Executioners*, p. 132.

27 A. Marwick, 'Review of P. Mandler, *History and National Life*', *History*, 88:1, no. 289, January 2003, pp. 84–6.

28 www.history.ac.uk/reviews/.

29 A. Perkins, *Red Queen: The Authorised Biography of Barbara Castle* (Pan, 2004), p. 111.

30 J. Haines, 'A Century of the People's Party', *Inside Labour: The New Labour Magazine*, February 2000, pp. 1–15.

31 K.O. Morgan, *Labour in Power 1945–1951* (Oxford University Press, 1989), p. 485.

32 Ibid.

33 E.P. Thompson, *The Making of the English Working Class* (Penguin, 1968) p. 10.

34 Ibid., p. 57.

35 Ibid., p. 39.

36 E.P. Thompson, 'Peculiarities of the English', in Thompson, *The Poverty of Theory* (Merlin, 1978), p. 62.

37 A. Munslow, 'Introduction: Theory and Practice', in A. Munslow and R. Rosenstone (eds), *Experiments in Rethinking History* (Routledge, 2004), p. 11.

38 L. Stone, 'History and Post-Modernism', *Past and Present*, 135, p. 193.

39 M. Foot, *Aneurin Bevan 1897–1945* (Paladin, 1975) p. 298.

40 R. Miliband, *Parliamentary Socialism* (Merlin, 1972), p. 269.

41 R. Spalding, 'Michael Foot: Myth and the Labour Left', *Socialist History*, 10, p. 29.

42 Perkins, *Red Queen: The Authorised Biography of Barbara Castle* (Pan, 2003), p. 63.

43 C. Parker, *The English Historical Tradition Since 1850* (John Donald, 1990), p. 95.

44 A. Thorpe, *A History of the British Labour Party* (Palgrave, 2001), p. 255.

45 R. Miliband, *Parliamentary Socialism* (Merlin, 1972), pp. 376–7.

46 D. Lipstadt, *Denying the Holocaust* (Penguin, 1994), p. 29.

47 'Rumsfeld steps up Iraq war talk', *Guardian*, 21 August 2002.

48 Ibid.

49 M. Housden, 'Intentionalist versus functionalist History', *Modern History Review*, November 1998, pp. 9–12.

50 Quoted in Dept. of Education and Science, *History in the Primary and*

Secondary Years: An HMI View (HMSO, 1985), p. 1.
51 A. Werth, *The Khrushchev Phase* (Robert Hale Ltd., 1961), p. 80.

5

Gender and history

Introduction

In a collection of essays published to mark the fortieth anniversary of the publication of E.H. Carr's *What is History?* David Cannadine stated that twenty-first century historians were less concerned with processes of change, than with meanings.[1] What he understood by this was that researchers no longer focus on developmental chains that attempt to explain the shaping of the present; rather, they seek to deconstruct the elements that mould the meaning of human institutions and activities. This new emphasis is clearly apparent in Cannadine's *Ornamentalism: How the British Saw their Empire*, where he states that he will investigate the British Empire as a place 'that both reflected and reinforced commonplace perceptions of the domestic social structure'.[2] Cannadine, in other words, viewed the Empire as a structure that served to buttress the meanings conveyed by British institutions. To illustrate this point one might contrast Cannadine's view of 'Ornamentalism', with Marxist accounts that interpreted the experience of Empire as a stage in Britain's economic development.[3]

Gender history can, perhaps, be seen as an example of the development outlined by Cannadine. It presents gender identities, of both men and women, as cultural and social constructs, as, in other words, bundles of meanings usually embodied in language. As the web site of the journal, *Gender & History* states:

> *Gender & History* aims to create productive debates and dialogues
> across subfields, historiographies, and theoretical orientations. It does
> so by publishing field-defining work on changing conceptions, prac-
> tices and semiotics of gender – femininities, masculinities and their
> historical contexts.[4]

The reference to semiotics is indicative of the influence of postmodernism on Gender historians. Semiotics is usually defined as
the science of signs, signs in this context meaning the conveyors of
significance, or meaning. Gender history did not spring into the
world fully formed, it was preceded by and grew out of an approach that focused on one gender, and viewed relationships between genders in terms of a dynamic historical process, this was
what was called 'Women's History'. This was a sub-discipline that
emerged out of the women's liberation movement of the late 1960s,
and one that had an explicitly political commitment which was to
understand women's situation in the present by uncovering the
historical trajectory of their oppression.[5] A key question that will
have to be considered here is what distinguishes these approaches
to history, and why and how the change of emphasis developed.
However, before doing that it is important to note that gender
historians share the broadly oppositional stance of Women's History. Denise Riley, for example, argues that her interest in the gender construction of women flows from her belief that language is
the location of women's oppression.[6] That shared oppositional stance
provides a useful starting point for a consideration of the context
that paved the way for the development of women's history.

Changing the world

It is very important that readers are clear that Women's History,
when capitalised at least, is not simply the history of women. It is,
rather, a historically based political programme, an assault on the
status quo. As such, its practitioners recognised that as their opponent, male-dominated society, often legitimised the status quo by
reference to tradition and historical precedent, then they too would
need to develop their own counter-history.[7] This process can be
seen at work in many moments of revolt in the past even in periods
of turbulence that were not initiated by the revolt of women.

For many centuries one of the most potent historical justifications for the marginalisation of women was provided by the biblical account of Adam and Eve's expulsion from the Garden of Eden. This fall from grace was held to be primarily the responsibility of Eve, the 'weaker vessel'. For succumbing to temptation God declared:

> I will greatly multiply thy sorrow and thy conception; in sorrow thou shalt bring forth children; and thy desire shall be to thy husband, and he shall rule over thee.[8]

Thus was the lot of women given divine sanction. This message was powerfully reinforced within Christian cultures for hundreds of years. One might, for example, read Shakespeare's *Macbeth*, where the lead character, urged on by his wife, murdered his king and seized the crown as warning of what might occur if wives were not 'ruled' by husbands. Shakespeare reinforced this point by having Macbeth defeated by Macduff, who was not 'of woman born', that is he was the product of a caesarian section, rather than a normal birth, and as such, a figure brought to life independently of a woman's body.[9]

The turmoil of the seventeenth-century English Revolution created an environment in which some, particularly the members of the many radical sects, began to question gender roles. 'Ranter' preachers promoted the right to free divorce, equal marriages and sexual freedom. To justify this 'revolution' they developed their own historical narrative, claiming that as they, through the overthrow of the King, had regained the state of grace lost by Adam, 'they may go naked as he did, and love above sin and shame'.[10] Hence, wives no longer needed to be ruled by their husbands, or solely subject to their sexual desires.

The French Revolution produced another outburst of radical iconoclasm. In 1791 the radical, Tom Paine published *Rights of Man*, a forthright defence of the French Revolution against the assault launched by Edmund Burke in his *Reflections on the Revolution in France*. Almost inevitably, given Burke's stress on the value of continuity, tradition and hereditary monarch, Paine put forward an alternative historical view, one which depicted the monarchy as the product of an act of robbery perpetrated by William the Conqueror in 1066.[11] The following year Mary Wollstonecraft took the debate in a different direction with the publication of *Vindication of the Rights of Women*. This combined support for the French Revolution with a passionate argument for women to be afforded the full rights of citizenship. Like the radicals of the seventeenth century, Wollstonecraft also called into question the institutions that regulated the lives of women; marriage, for example, she described as 'legal prostitution'. Like Paine she also set her analysis in a historical framework. Within this, society moves through a number of stages beginning with barbarism and moving on to monarchy. As human culture develops, two contradictory developments occur: the power of the human mind grows, but at the same time society became increasingly dominated by parasitic despots. However, this situation produces its own solution, 'the nature of the poison points the antidote' and although Wollstonecraft doesn't actually use the term, one can reasonably assume that the 'antidote' is revolution, out of which comes 'the perfection of man in the establishment of true civilisation'.[12] Wollstonecraft uses the term 'man' to mean humanity, and thus the 'true civilisation' that she envisaged was one in which women could assume the role of full citizens.

Challenges to the political and social status quo have often, then, led to the development of challenges to traditional views of the female role. Such challenges have frequently also led to the development of new historical narratives, albeit often of a fairly rudimentary nature. Such connections can best be understood as the response to the value placed on women's subservient and domestic role by the socially conservative, as in the following quotation:

> In the male the moral effects of the system are very sad, but in the female they are infinitely worse, not alone upon themselves, but upon their families, upon society, and I may add upon the country itself. It is bad enough if you corrupt the man, but if you corrupt the woman, you poison the waters of life at the very fountain.[13]

For Lord Shaftesbury, speaking in the 1840s on the employment of women in coalmines, the removal of wives and mothers from the domestic sphere threatened the very foundations of society.

Given these linkages it is not surprising that the most radical critics of nineteenth-century society, Karl Marx and Friedrich Engels, should have turned their attention to the question of the family and the role of women. In *The Origin of the Family, Private Property and the State*, Engels argued that monogamous marriage was a product of the development of private property. Prior to this development, he argued, early societies had been matriarchal with descent passing down the female line. As agriculture led to the accumulation, for the first time, of significant levels of property, Engels argued men felt moved to secure this inheritance by replacing matriarchal with patriarchal inheritance and enforcing monogamy on their wives, to place the security of their line beyond doubt.[14] This development had the effect of turning marriage into a primarily economic arrangement; a relationship that Engels both characterised as the first class conflict and, like Wollstonecraft, 'the crassest prostitution'.[15] The institution of marriage was also, in Engels's view, rotten with hypocrisy in that it required the monogamy of the wife, but not of the husband. Given the link made by Engels between the origins of private property and the unequal, oppressive nature of marriage, it was logical for him to claim that marriage could only become an equal partnership after the abolition of private property following the socialist revolution.[16] Engels's work was particularly influential on the exponents of Women's History who emerged in the 1960s and 1970s as he appeared to provide a historically based link between the oppression of the working class and the oppression of women.[17]

Pioneer historians

The figures that we have considered so far are not really historians, as such, but analysts and activists who rooted their work in a historical context. As we move into the twentieth century we begin to encounter figures who can be properly identified as historians, although they do come from what might be regarded as a broadly feminist background. Alice Clark, for example, was educated at the London School of Economics, which was established by the Fabian socialists Sidney and Beatrice Webb, and was closely associated with the labour movement. Thus Clark's education and commitment to the cause of women's suffrage locate her within an early twentieth-century radical milieu. Her political priorities also clearly informed her historical work. In her 1919 work, *Working Life of Women in the Seventeenth Century*, for example, at several points she stated that her historical work had significance for the study of sociology, in other words that it enhanced the under-standing of life in Clark's own time.[18]

Clark's central argument was that when work of all kinds was centred on the home, the wife played a part as an equal partner in the production of the family income. During the course of the seventeenth century, she further claimed, there was the beginning of a tendency to separate domestic and working spaces, which had a number of negative effects: firstly, that the labour market came to be dominated by men, with women enjoying such benefits as work conferred only via the indulgence of their husband. Secondly, that women could no longer be employed in their husband's occu-pation. Finally, women belonging to the better-off sections of the commercial classes withdrew from business entirely.[19] Many women became confined in a state of 'domestic slavery'.[20] Women also ex-perienced a loss of educational opportunities. As late as 1914, when Vera Brittain secured a place at Somerville College, Oxford, her mother was assailed by friends asking: 'How can you send your daughter to college, Mrs. Brittain … don't you want her ever to get *married*?'[21] Many other middle-class women were condemned, according to Clark, to a life of domestic idleness.[22] As Beatrice Webb recalled, looking back on her own privileged late Victorian background:

> According to the current code, the entire time and energy of an un-married daughter … was assumed to be spent, either in serving the family group, or in entertaining and being entertained by the social circle to which she belonged.[23]

Clark's analysis of the seventeenth century sought to uncover the origins of the conditions under which women lived in the early twentieth century.[24] She argued that the processes which separated home from work, and at the same time led to the social marginalisation of women, were the product of the development of capitalism. The connection between economic development and the status of women was one that would be taken up by the exponents of Women's History later in the twentieth century. However, Clark's view of capitalism was not that it had to be overthrown, but rather modified by the increased participation of women. This view flowed from her belief that capitalism had produced a State 'which regards the purpose of life solely from the male standpoint'. Such a society was characterised by 'instability, superficiality and spiritual poverty'. The solution to such a situation was 'the organisation of the whole, which is both male and female'.[25] The emancipation of women would therefore immeasurably improve the quality of society; this view is perhaps similar in some ways to the connection made by Mary Wollstonecraft between 'civilisation' and full citizenship for women.

As well as pioneering the idea that a connection existed between women's status and economic development, Clark also touched upon other areas that would be taken up by later generations. In her introductory chapter, for example, Clark tackled the idea that women had certain fixed characteristics, an idea which she completely rejected:

> This assumption has however no basis in fact, for the most superficial consideration will show how profoundly women can be changed by their environment.[26]

This is interesting because it could be seen as pre-figuring the idea, developed by gender historians, that female identity is a social construct that changes over time, rather than a fixed biological entity. After completing her book Clark returned to work for the family firm, and her influence as an historian seems to have been limited in the early twentieth century. She was nevertheless important as one of the first feminists who combined activism with academically rigorous historical work.

Ivy Pinchbeck's *Women Workers and the Industrial Revolution 1750–1850*, first published in 1930, is another important pioneering text. Pinchbeck, like Clark saw the advance of industrialisation as furthering the separation of home and work, however, she drew rather different conclusions about the effects of this process. Working-class women factory workers, Pinchbeck argued, enjoyed 'higher wages, better food and clothing and an improved standard of living'.[27] She also claimed that factory work enhanced women's 'self-respect, self-reliance and courage'.[28] For Pinchbeck, the fact that some married women were confined to the domestic sphere as a result of industrialisation was also a beneficial development.

> In this sense the industrial revolution marked a real advance, since it led to the assumption that men's wages should be paid on a family basis, and prepared the way for the more modern conception that in the rearing of children and in home-making, the married woman makes an adequate economic contribution.[29]

This sounds rather conservative in tone, but it was not totally at odds with early twentieth-century feminism. Alice Clark had deplored the idea that women should be solely concerned with domestic life, but she had also described 'the spiritual creation of the home and the physical creation of the child' as 'the highest, most intense forms to which women's energy is directed'.[30] One could perhaps see both writers wrestling with, without fully articulating it, 'the tension between the plea for equality and the assertion of sexual difference'.[31] The difficulty, that is, of striking a balance between the desire for equal treatment and the recognition that real differences do exist between the genders. This is an issue that is articulated later in the twentieth century, and is one to which we will return later in this chapter.

Pinchbeck agreed with Clark that one of the consequences of the separation of home from work was a regime of enforced idleness for middle-class women. However, she goes on to argue that the example of independent working-class women inspired some middle-class women to begin challenging their conventional roles by the end of the nineteenth century.[32] Pinchbeck's argument was essentially that the entry of increasing numbers of women into the labour market was the road to their emancipation.[33] In some respects this view resembles Marxist accounts, which saw the route to liberation for women as via their transformation into class-conscious proletarians.[34] Pinchbeck though, saw entry into the labour market as liberating in itself, not as a prelude to the proletarian revolution. Later women's historians have challenged her 'optimistic' account of the Industrial Revolution. Pat Hudson has claimed that those, like Pinchbeck, who stress the importance of labour market participation fail to note that 'many forces combined to structure and restructure the nature of patriarchy and female subordination over time'.[35] Ultimately, the main significance of Pinchbeck's and Clark's work is that by writing women into the historical record, they legitimised their experience as a subject for historical investigation, and laid the basis for subsequent developments.

Women's historians and the 1960s

In the post-Second World War period the numbers of students entering universities greatly increased. Although still outnumbered by men this also involved an absolute increase in the numbers of women entering higher education. Before 1939, particularly at the ancient universities, undergraduate life was about confirming one's status within the ruling and administrative elite.[36] The students of the 1960s, lacking private incomes, viewed their education as vital to their career prospects; at the same time university expansion was specifically related to the state's economic needs. This situation produced, in some students, a feeling that the humane values promoted by universities were at odds with their ultimate career destinations. This feeling of alienation, particularly when combined with threatening international developments, like the development of nuclear weapons and the Vietnam War, tended to move significant number of students towards the political left. So strong was this development that some student 'theorists' described the universities as 'Red Bases' of socialism within capitalist societies.[37] This was the milieu from which emerged the women's liberation movement. This in turn produced the Women's Historians of the 1960s.[38]

Given the situation from which they emerged, it is perhaps not surprising that these historians saw their historical work as intimately connected with their political beliefs, and were heavily influenced by Marxism. This was the case with Sheila Rowbotham, both a university-trained historian and a pioneer of the women's liberation movement. The concerns that inform Rowbotham's early work were clearly laid out in an article that she published in 1970. There, she noted women are 'absolutely essential to the community as producers and consumers. But they don't produce things and they don't get paid, so capitalism does not value them'.[39] What is apparent here is a desire to relate the subordination of women to the needs of the capitalist mode of production. Not surprisingly, Rowbotham saw the way forward as participation in the class struggle. Women, she argued, who took such a course 'break through all the hopelessness, all the fatality, the resignation, the passivity'.[40] These ideas were elaborated in a small book, published in 1973, where Rowbotham also touched on a number of historical themes. The nuclear family of the twentieth century was, she claimed, a product of industrialisation, when (here she follows on from Alice Clark) the workplace was separated from the home, a development which tended to limit women to the domestic sphere. She also noted that this separation of spheres and the domestic subordination of women was presented as a natural occurrence.[41]

Given this perspective it is perhaps not surprising that Rowbotham should have turned to history to strengthen her political analysis. Her ground-breaking *Hidden from History* came, as she put it 'very directly from a political movement'.[42] She acknowledged that the oppression of women pre-dated capitalism, but that capitalism had given that oppression a particular form, a form which persisted down to the late twentieth century.[43] According to Rowbotham, by the end of the nineteenth century the specific features of the capitalist oppression of women were in place and consisted of: unrewarded and unrecognised labour in the home, producing and maintaining, in a literal sense, the labour force; disadvantaged access to the labour market through low-paid occupations; and a consequent economic dependence on men.[44]

By demonstrating the historical development of the capitalist oppression of women, Rowbotham sought to undermine the idea that this sexual division of labour was in some senses inevitable. Her work also sought to point to ways of dealing with this situation by highlighting the activism of women in the past. The idea that one could influence the politics of the present by 'recovering' a lost tradition of political radicalism was a common one in the late 1960s and 1970s. It certainly influenced the feminist publishing house, Virago, established in 1973, which republished works like *The Hard Way Up*, the autobiography of Hannah Mitchell, a working-class suffragette and labour movement activist.[45]

Rowbotham's historical work had a clear political purpose, to demonstrate how the current oppression of women developed. It also sets out to offer a way to overthrow that oppression. Given that Rowbotham's historical work attempts to integrate an account of women's oppression into a Marxist schema, it is not surprising that she saw her narrative as ending in a process of 'revolutionary reawakening' that began in 1968.

> Women's liberation is part of this awakening and a socialist feminism is again possible in the world. Such beginnings though are very fragile and the fortunes of the new feminism will depend on our capacity to relate to the working class and the action of working-class women in transforming women's liberation according to their needs.[46]

Rowbotham does, though, recognise that certain experiences are specific to women and that these raise issues about women's consciousness that cannot be resolved simply by incorporating women into the class struggle for socialism. These are questions that relate to the way specific aspects of women's lives are dealt with in a male world: 'We are continually translating our own immediate fragmented sense of what we feel into a framework which is constructed by men.'[47] It was precisely the difficulty of dealing with such areas of women's experience that led some researchers to argue that the issue that needed dealing with was not, or not just, capitalism, but patriarchy, by which they meant institutionalised male power. Women historians operating within this frame of reference tended to investigate different areas from socialist feminists, like Rowbotham. They often focused on institutions and practices that in their view embodied and sustained male power, such as male violence against women, rape and marriage.[48] A good example of this approach is contained in a collection of essays, *The Sexual Dynamics of History*, published in 1983. In this work the collectively authored introduction rejected the class-based constraints of Marxism, and declared: 'It is time to add the missing dynamic in history – men's power and women's resistance'.[49] The central argument here is that a key force in history is the conflict between the sexes, a struggle which, it is claimed, waxes and wanes as historical circumstances change and levels of women's resistance rise and fall. Other important elements in this analysis are that all men benefit from the oppression of women; 'the oppression of women is often conscious and deliberate'; and that consequently all women have a common interest in resisting male oppression.[50]

Using this perspective, radical feminist historians reinterpreted a wide range of developments and phenomena relating to women. Freud at the end of the nineteenth century, for example, had claimed that hysteria in young women was often the product of sexual anxiety, particularly as they approached marriage. He also claimed that such hysterias 'vanish if in the course of time sexual enjoyment emerges and wipes out the trauma'.[51] Or, to put this another way, the cure for some forms of hysteria was a 'normal' heterosexual sex life. Against this, the authors of *The Sexual Dynamics of History* assert that, in the past, hysteria had been a form of resistance to male power, one of the mechanisms of which was heterosexuality.[52]

Adopting the perspective of a 'sex war' as opposed to a class war enabled such radical feminist historians to reinterpret a range of behaviours that might in the past have simply seemed the product of individual aberrations. Hence instances of women dressing and living as men, a common enough phenomenon to be recorded in folk song, was also represented as a strategy employed by women in the conflict with male oppressors.[53] On a larger scale, Sheila Jeffreys' contribution claimed that sexology, the 'scientific' investigation of sexual practices, that emerged in the early twentieth century, was in reality an ideological development that sought to counter the development of feminism by defining heterosexuality as the norm for sexual activity. Against this Jeffreys argued:

> The heterosexual couple is a political relationship within which the woman's labour is extracted and the woman's life is controlled and harnessed to the satisfaction of man's needs.[54]

This particular historical dynamic did pose certain problems. It seemed, for example, to preclude totally the possibility of equal heterosexual relationships; indeed, it was stated that lesbianism was 'one of the strongest forms of resistance' to male power.[55] It also seemed to imply a conflict that could never be resolved for as long as humanity was divided into two sexes. These points were raised in a short essay, taking issue with the concept of patriarchy, written by Sheila Rowbotham, in the early 1980s.[56] The essay was answered by two other socialist feminist historians, Sally Alexander and Barbara Taylor, who argued, as had many women before them, that class-based analyses were not sufficient to understand the role of men and women in society, but more importantly, that sex roles were socially, not biologically determined.[57] From this perspective Patriarchy was not an eternal structure, but a useful tool with which to analyse those aspects of male/female interaction that could not be satisfactorily examined using the Marxist model alone. What eventually emerged from this interaction between the various branches of feminist history was what we now know as gender history. This is an approach that focuses on the social and ideological construction of both male and female identities. Socialist feminist and radical feminist historians had touched the issue of the social production of gender identities, but it was only through a process of interaction and debate that the approach became fully articulated.

Gender historians

Catherine Hall's starting point for her investigation of the development of Birmingham's middle class in the early nineteenth century was, like Alice Clark's, the separation of domestic and working spaces. Her argument was that up until the late eighteenth century many wives of businessmen played a full and active part in the family enterprise. As businesses developed and prospered, she argued, women increasingly withdrew to the domestic sphere. Hall does not simply regret the inactivity that this separation enforced on middle-class women, she argued instead that this process led to the development of new and distinctive male and female identities. The identity of the successful businessman would be based both on his ownership of property and his public role within a range of commercial, political and cultural organisations.[58] Women, on the other hand were mainly confined to the home; in those rare instances when they did participate in public life, they did so in such a way that pointed up specific feminine qualities. Hence, appeals to support the anti-slavery movement were directed to them 'as mothers to save their "dusky sisters" from having their children torn from them'.[59] This sense of constructing an identity is clearly apparent in the many guides to etiquette and household management that were published in the nineteenth century. In the most famous of these Isabella Beeton declared:

> As with the commander of an army, or the leader of any enterprise, so it is with the mistress of a house. Her spirit will be seen through the whole establishment ... Of all these acquirements, which more particularly belong to the feminine character, there are none which take a higher rank, in our estimation, than such as enter into a knowledge of household duties.[60]

Such domestic administration was not, then, simply a woman's duty; it was, in Beeton's view, an expression of 'feminine character', an intrinsic quality.

Hall's analysis, which she extended in collaboration with Leonore Davidoff, integrated the social construction of gender identities with the development of social classes. Indeed, they stated in the Prologue of *Family Fortunes: Men and Women of the English middle class 1780–1850*: 'The principal argument rests on the assumption that gender and class always operate together, that consciousness of class always takes a gendered form.'[61] The approach embodied here provides, because the emphasis is on social construction, a dynamic model of development that is not 'fixed' by biology. The approach also would appear to owe something to the 'cultural' approach to social history, pioneered by E.P. Thompson in *The Making of the English Working Class*.[62] Unlike Thompson, though, Davidoff and Hall have produced a gendered account, that is, one that recognised that men and women experience social developments in significantly different ways. They both also have backgrounds, as they acknowledge within the women's liberation movement and the socialist historiography that began to develop in Britain in the 1960s. Their approach to gender does not, therefore, represent a radical break with earlier socialist feminists, but a development from it.

Similar linkages are apparent, and acknowledged in Judith Walkowitz's *City of Dreadful Delight*, a work which focused on the

'Jack the Ripper' murders as a way of exploring the interactions of class and gender in late Victorian culture. In her account 'the prostitute' became:

> the embodiment of the corporeal smells and animal passions that the rational bourgeois male had repudiated and that the virtuous woman, the spiritualized 'angel in the house,' had suppressed.[63]

Part, therefore, of the significance of responses to the 'Ripper' cases, was in Walkowitz's view, the light that was shed on the construction of Victorian gender identities. The passionless 'virtue' of the idealised Victorian household was sustained by the expulsion of sensuality into the brothel and on to the street, the resorts of the intensely physical prostitute. Just as E.P. Thompson argued that class identity could only be defined by examining the relationship between classes, so Walkowitz argued that gender identities have to be defined in the same way. Or, to put this another way, the virtuous middle-class wife is only recognisable as such because she does not have the earthy attributes of the lower-class woman, the fullest embodiment of which was the prostitute. This did not prevent the working-class woman becoming an object of desire for the middle-class man, but that desire was either expressed voyeuristically or in particular spheres, away from the home. Walkowitz noted that social investigations, worthy activities on one level, often had this voyeuristic quality.[64] This is clearly apparent in the following extract dealing with the employment of young girls in textile factories:

> Here ... will be found an utter absence of grace and feminine manners – a peculiar timbre of voice – no such thing as speaking soft and low, 'that most excellent thing in woman', a peculiarity owing to various causes, a principal one of which is, too much sexual excitement, producing a state of vocal organs closely resembling that of the male.[65]

In this extract it is quite clear how Peter Gaskell, the author, defines factory girls in terms of their lack of middle-class feminine attributes. He also, incidentally, sheds light on aspects of middle-class male identity, as there are clear indications that he is physically attracted to these girls, suggesting that the sexual excitement was probably his, rather than theirs'.

Walkowitz, although writing from an academic standpoint, still wrote with half an eye on the present, in that she expressed the belief that lessons could be learnt from the past.

> Today, as in the past, feminists struggle to devise an effective strategy to combat sexual violence and humiliation … In this cultural milieu, we feminists have to come to grips with the painful historic contradictions of feminist sexual strategies not only for the sex workers … but for ourselves.[66]

This passage indicates that Walkowitz views history as a progressive process and, more significantly, acknowledges that there is an entity called the past that can be accessed through history. This last point may seem terribly obvious but it is important because it marks her off from the postmodernist historians that we will shortly consider.

One change that was wrought by the development of Gender History was that men became as much the object of attention as women. Furthermore, this development enabled men to enter into a field that had largely been dominated by women. In this respect, it is important to mention John Tosh's 1999 work, *A Man's Place: Masculinity and the Middle-Class Home in Victorian England.* This examination of the construction of masculinity covers similar territory to Hall and Davidoff, although over a different time-span.[67] His central argument is that the Victorian middle-class male identity was essentially shaped by the increasing importance of the domestic sphere, within which clear and distinctive gender roles were performed. Finally, as a historian whose academic development was influenced by Marxism, it is perhaps not surprising that Tosh should argue that the events of the past continued to exercise an influence on the present: 'The Victorians articulated an ideal of home life against which men's conduct has been measured ever since'.[68]

Gender historians and postmodernism

All of the gender historians cited above viewed gender identities as expressions of social change within a wider society, that, to put it another way, such changes were the product of processes within a wider, external world. Furthermore, they also placed their works within a framework of continuing development. During the course of the 1980s a number of historians emerged who rejected the notion that language described and referred to a separate sphere of experience. Such historians, applying the approaches pioneered by figures like Michel Foucault, rejected the view that language referred to a separate reality, in favour of the idea that language was the only reality. As Gareth Stedman Jones put it:

> I became increasingly critical of the prevalent treatment of the 'social' as something outside of, and logically – and often, though not necessarily, chronologically – prior to its articulation through language.[69]

As a consequence Stedman Jones began to treat class 'as a discursive rather than as an ontological reality',[70] by which he meant that he treated 'class' as a linguistic term that stimulated a range of cultural and political associations, also framed within language, rather than a social structure with an external existence. It is difficult to suggest with precision what the context for this transformation – from Marxist to postmodernist – was, but it is surely significant that he should cite Eric Hobsbawm's *The Forward March of Labour Halted* (1981) as one of the starting points for his reconsideration. Hobsbawm's work suggested, in the aftermath of Margaret Thatcher's 1979 General Election triumph, that the traditional Marxist view of class politics had failed and was no longer a useful model. In that light the espousal of postmodernism might be seen as the product of the defeat of that political tradition, a defeat apparently confirmed by the collapse of communism in Eastern Europe between 1989–91.

Some gender historians were also drawn into the orbit of postmodernism. Both Joan Scott and Denise Riley have, for example, argued that terms like 'man', 'woman' and 'women' have no objective existence outside of language. They also argue that the discursive nature of such terms means that they have a fluid and fluctuating nature, which changes over time.[71] Riley also argues that such terms do not even mean the same thing to everybody at specific moments. People, it is stated, have multiple identities, and can select the ones that they wish to promote.

While you might choose to take on being a disabled person or a les-
bian, for instance, as a political position, you might not elect to make
a politics out of other designations. As you do not live your life fully
defined as a shop assistant, nor do you as a Greek Cypriot, for example, and you can always refute such identifications in the name of
another description which, because it is more individuated, may ring
more truthfully to you.[72]

This view raises a number of crucial issues. Firstly, it appears to
dissolve the possibility of solidarity between women, if the existence of such an entity is accepted, because potentially they could
assume such a wide disparity of identities. Secondly, it seems to
imply that identities are not socially shaped, but individually chosen: that, to a large degree one can shape one's own identity, and
this appears to flow from the rejection of the idea that any reality
might exist beyond language. However, Riley does argue that the
construction of 'women' changes over time, as a consequence of the
're-ordering' of other ideas, like 'Nature'. This process, which began in the seventeenth century, is framed in very general terms
that involved the re-ordering of the understanding of gender.[73]
This process appears to imply a collective experience, but why, we
might wonder, should it, as Riley argues individuals can, by stress-
ing different aspects of their identity, respond to any given historical situation in a multiplicity of ways? Riley's problem, one suspects,
is that her historical analysis requires a motive force to explain
generalised change, which it would be extremely difficult to construct without some sense of collective responses.

Riley and Scott both see themselves in the feminist tradition,
but believe that the oppression of women resides in the linguistic
construction of the term 'Women', because oppression is an essential part of the discourse of this term. Riley argues that the purpose of historical work is to dissolve this identity of 'Women' and
replace it with the more inclusive identity of humanity. The problem with this objective is that 'Humanity' can also be seen as a
contested discourse. Humanity, created in God's image, is a very
different entity for the creationist than it is for either the Darwin-
ian, or the Freudian. The postmodernists have played a major role
in demonstrating the power of language to shape meaning. Notions

like 'Discourse' have also developed an awareness of how concepts and ideas are embedded in webs of meaning and associations. However, despite such gains, the postmodernist historian is still confronted with the problems of causation and destination. In a situation in which all experience is contained within language, what actually brings about changes in meaning? Similarly, if there is nothing beyond language, then any designated 'destination' for historical development will always be prone to dissolve into a mass of contested definitions.

Conclusion

In any brief account of an intellectual development there is, almost inevitably, a tendency to produce an overly linear narrative. Consequently it might seem from the above that socialist and radical feminist histories have given way to postmodernist influenced gender-based interpretations. So to avoid that it is necessary to point out that the development of a new historical approach does not automatically lead to the extinction of all previous approaches. For example, in 1995 Jane Purvis put forward a number of trenchant criticisms of the approaches developed by Denise Riley and Joan Wallach Scott. Their analysis, she claimed, did not study women as women, but as social constructs. In the process, she further claimed, it meant that women were no longer seen as historical agents; in other words they did not act, but simply were. Gender studies, because it included the study of masculinity, tended to sideline women, she argued; and by arguing for a multiplicity of masculinities, such practices denied the existence of Patriarchy as an oppressive construct.[74] Not all Women's historians react quite so strongly against the development of Gender Studies; Joanne Bailey, for example, argues that both approaches can be mutually beneficial; however, the argument that practitioners from both camps can learn from one another does rest on the belief that they should nevertheless continue their separate existences. In other words, Women's History in this view cannot be subsumed, into Gender Studies.[75]

Like all other fields of historical activity Women's History and Gender History were formed within particular contexts. Bearing this in mind, one might see the development of postmodernist approaches that deny the existence of spheres of experience outside of language, and which reject the notion of progress and direction in history, as reflecting, however indirectly, the defeat of Soviet Communism and the apparent triumph of western social and economic values. One can even point to writers, particularly in the United States, who argue for a 'struggle-free' feminism, within which one can make one's own identity. In 1999 Elizabeth Wutzel published *Bitch: In Praise of Difficult Women*, in which she stated, 'I have a tough time feeling that feminism has done a damn bit of good, if I can't be the way I am.' The type of identity that Wurtzel wished to be recognised was perhaps indicated by her appearance naked, on the cover of the book. In the same book she claimed:

> The reluctance that many women feel in saying that they are feminists is understandable; they feel alienated from the label because they feel it puts them in some sort of a ghetto, that it defines them as an activist or a socialist or a lesbian or somebody who is humourless or dowdy or celibate.[76]

Wurtzel's position appears to be one that wishes to equate feminism with any form of assertive female behaviour, regardless of content. Critics might argue that such a view is underpinned by the kind of argument advanced by Denise Riley about selecting one's identity.

Although one might see the development of postmodern approaches to gender history as related to the collapse of Communism there is a crucial difference between this development and the marginalisation of Marxism. When the Soviet Union disappeared, for many that meant the disappearance of the tangible evidence for Marxism, and also for concepts like class struggle. However, feminism was rooted in a different reality, that of the multiple disabilities that women suffer in society. While such a situation persists, women will continue to debate and discuss how to deal with it, and in struggling to come to terms with the present they will logically, as this chapter has argued, continue to grapple with the past and out of that situation will come conflicting interpretations. The final point that we can make is, therefore, that the situation regarding women's and gender history is likely to be one of constant change, and development.

Further reading

Downs, Laura Lee, *Writing Gender History* (Oxford University Press, 2005).

Hall, C., *White, Male and Middle Class: Explorations in Feminism and History* (Polity Press, 1992).

Kessler Harris, A., 'What is Gender History now?', in D. Cannadine, *What is History Now?* (Palgrave Macmillan, 2002).

Purvis, J. (ed.), *Women's History, Britain 1850–1945* (UCL Press, 1995).

Riley, D., *Am I That Name? Feminism and the Category of 'Women' in History* (Macmillan, 1988).

Rowbotham, S., *Hidden from History* (Pluto Press, 1992).

Wallach Scott, J., *Gender and the Politics of History* (Columbia University Press, 1999).

Notes

1 D. Cannadine, *What is History Now?* (Palgrave Macmillan, 2002), pp. xi–xii.

2 D. Cannadine, *Ornamentalism: How the British Saw their Empire* (Allen Lane, 2001), p. xx.

3 T. Kemp, *Industrialization in Nineteenth Century Europe* (Longman, 1971), p. 193.

4 www.blackwellpublishing.com/aims.asp?ref=0953–5233, accessed 13 February 2007.

5 S. Rowbotham, *Hidden From History* (Pluto Press, 1974), p. ix.

6 D. Riley, *Am I That Name? Feminism and the Category of 'Women' in History* (Macmillan, 1988), p. 3.

7 'In a class society history has meant the history of the rulers, and in a male dominated society the history of men.' A. Davin, quoted in C. Hall, *White, Male and Middle Class: Explorations in Feminism and History* (Polity Press, 1992), p. 8.

8 Genesis, 3.16, King James Authorised Version of the Bible.

9 W. Shakespeare, *Macbeth*, Act V, Scene VIII.

10 Quoted in C. Hill, *The World Turned Upside Down* (Pelican, 1975), p. 317.

11 E. Burke, *Reflections on the Revolution in France*. First published 1790 (Pelican, 1968), p. 119; T. Paine, *Rights of Man*. First published 1791 (Everyman, 1969), p. 163.

12 M. Wollstonecraft, *Vindication of the Rights of Woman*. First published 1792 (Penguin, 1982), pp. 98–9.

13 Lord Shaftesbury, quoted in I. Pinchbeck, *Women Workers in the Industrial Revolution* (Virago, 1981), p. 267.

14 F. Engels, *The Origin of the Family, Private Property and the State*. First published in German in 1884 (Pathfinder, 1972) p. 90.

15 Ibid., p. 99 and p. 105 respectively.

16 Ibid., p. 116.

17 E. Reed, Introduction, in F. Engels, *The Origin of the Family, Private Property and the State*, p. 9.

18 A. Clark, *Working Life of Women in the Seventeenth Century*. First published 1919 (Frank Cass, 1968), p. 2.

19 Ibid., p. 296.

20 M. Spring Rice, *Working Class Wives*. First published 1939 (Virago 1981), p. 14.

21 V. Brittain, *Testament of Youth* (Fontana, 1979), p. 72.

22 M. Vicinus, *Independent Women: Work and Community for Single Women 1850–1920* (Virago, 1985), p.13.

23 B. Webb, *My Apprenticeship* (Longmans, Green and Co., 1926), p. 116.

24 A. Clark, Preface, *Working Life of Women in the Seventeenth Century*.

25 Ibid., p. 308.

26 Ibid., p. 1.

27 I. Pinchbeck, *Women Workers and the Industrial Revolution 1750–1850*. First published 1930 (Virago, 1981), p. 311.

28 Ibid., p. 308.

29 Ibid., pp. 312–13.

30 Clark, *Working Life of Women in the Seventeenth Century*, p. 4.

31 S. Alexander, 'Women, class and sexual difference in the 1830s and 1840s: Some reflections on the writing of a feminist history', *History Workshop Journal*, 17, Spring 1984, p. 126.

32 Pinchbeck, *Women Workers and the Industrial Revolution*, pp. 315–16.

33 Ibid., Preface to the 1968 edition.

34 E. Marx Aveling, Second Report on the Gotha Congress of the German SPD, *Justice*, 7 November 1896, available at: http://marxists.org/archive/eleanor-marx/1896/10gotha.html#zetkin.

35 P. Hudson, 'Women and Industrialization', in Jane Purvis (ed.), *Women's History: Britain 1850–1945* (UCL Press, 1995), p. 25.

36 R. Hilary, *The Last Enemy* (Macmillan & Co., 1943), p. 10.

37 A. Cockburn, 'Introduction', in A. Cockburn and R. Blackburn (eds), *Student Power: Problems, Diagnosis, Action* (Penguin, 1969), p. 17.

38 S. Rowbotham, *Woman's Consciousness, Man's World* (Penguin, 1973), p. 17; S. Alexander, 'Women, class and sexual differences in the 1830s and 1840s',

History Workshop Journal, 17, Spring 1984, p. 127; Hall, *White, Male and Middle Class*, p. 3.

39 S. Rowbotham, 'Cinderella Organizes Buttons', *Black Dwarf,* 1970, reproduced in D. Widgery (ed.), *The Left in Britain 1956–68* (Penguin, 1976), p. 417.

40 Ibid., p. 420.

41 Rowbotham, *Woman's Consciousness, Man's World,* p. 57.

42 S. Rowbotham, *Hidden from History* (Pluto Press, 1974), p. ix.

43 Ibid., p. x.

44 Ibid., pp. 58–9.

45 H. Mitchell, *The Hard Way Up* (Virago, 1977). For details of Virago, see www.virago.co.uk/virago/virago/history.asp?TAG=&CID=virago.

46 Rowbotham, *Hidden From History*, pp. 168–9.

47 S. Rowbotham, *Woman's Consciousness, Man's World* (Penguin, 1973) p.35.

48 J. Purvis, 'From "women worthies" to poststructuralism? Debate and controversy in women's history in Britain', in J. Purvis (ed.), *Women's History, Britain 1850–1945* (UCL Press, 1995), p. 10.

49 The London Feminist History Group, *The Sexual Dynamics of History* (Pluto Press, 1983), p. 3.

50 Ibid., pp. 4–6.

51 J. Breuer and Sigmund Freud, 'Studies on Hysteria', *The Standard Edition of the Complete Psychological Works of Sigmund Freud*, Vol. II (1893–1895) (The Hogarth Press Ltd, 1955), p. 246.

52 London Feminist History Group, *The Sexual Dynamics of History*, p. 6.

53 Ibid. See also 'The Female Drummer', in Roy Palmer (ed.), *The Rambling Soldier* (Penguin, 1977), pp. 163–4.

54 S. Jeffreys, 'Sex reform and anti-feminism in the 1920s', in London Feminist History Group, *The Sexual Dynamics of History*, p. 178. See also M. Jackson, *The Real Facts of Life: Feminism and the Politics of Sexuality c.1850–1940* (Taylor and Francis, 1994), pp. 106–29.

55 London Feminist History Group, *The Sexual Dynamics of History*, p. 6.

56 S. Rowbotham, 'The Trouble with "Patriarchy"', in R. Samuel (ed.), *People's History and Socialist Theory* (Routledge & Kegan Paul, 1981), pp. 364–9.

57 S. Alexander and B. Taylor, 'In Defence of "Patriarchy"', in Samuel (ed.), *People's History and Socialist Theory*, pp. 370–2.

58 C. Hall, 'Gender divisions and class formation in the Birmingham middle class 1780–1850', in R. Samuel (ed.), *People's History and Socialist Theory*, p. 170.

59 Ibid., p. 171.

60 I. Beeton, *Beeton's Book of Household Management.* First published 1861

(Jonathan Cape, 1968), p. 1.

61 L. Davidoff and C. Hall, *Family Fortunes: Men and women of the English middle class* (Hutchinson, 1987), p. 13.

62 E.P. Thompson, *The Making of the English Working Class* (Penguin, 1968), p. 10.

63 J.R. Walkowitz, *City of Dreadful Delight* (Virago, 1992), p. 21.

64 Ibid., pp. 20–1.

65 P. Gaskell, *The Manufacturing Population of England* (1833), pp. 162–4, in E. Royston Pike, *Human Documents of the Industrial Revolution* (George Allen & Unwin, 1966), p. 221.

66 Walkowitz, *City of Dreadful Delight*, p. 244.

67 J. Tosh, *A Man's Place: Masculinity and the Middle-Class Home in Victorian England* (Yale University Press, 1999), p. xi.

68 Ibid., pp. 7–8.

69 G. Stedman Jones, *Languages of Class 1832–1982* (Cambridge University Press, 1983), p. 7.

70 Ibid., p. 8.

71 Riley, *Am I That Name?*, p. 3; J. Wallach Scott, *Gender and the Politics of History* (Columbia University Press, 1999), p. 49.

72 Riley, *Am I That Name?*, p. 16.

73 Ibid., p. 14.

74 J. Purvis, 'From "women worthies" to poststructuralism? Debate and controversy in women's history in Britain', in Jane Purvis (ed.), *Women's History, Britain 1850–1945* (UCL Press, 1995), pp. 12–13.

75 J. Bailey, 'Is the rise of gender history "hiding" women from history once again?', *History in Focus: Articles on Gender History*, web site of the Institute of Historical Research, www.history.ac.uk/ihr/Focus/Gender/articles.html.

76 Quoted by K. Gorton, 'A New Time For Feminism: "Then and Now"', www.feminist-seventies.net/Gorton.html, accessed 13 February 2007.

6

Historiography and the Nazis

Introduction

In 2005, the Historical Association (HA) published a government-sponsored report, which attacked what it referred to as the 'Hitlerisation' of history. In its analysis the report made two related points: firstly that Nazi Germany was over-represented in the school curriculum for the post-14 age group, and secondly, that this over-representation made school students, at best, negative about, and at worst, positively hostile towards, modern Germans. The report's positive reference to what *The Spectator* called 'Our shameful Nazi fetish', helped to conjure a picture of the mindless anti-German 'patriotism' that characterises elements of British society, and is most apparent in the violent exploits of some football supporters.[1] However much we may deplore such attitudes and activities, as students of historiography we are still faced with a question which the HA report does not address, which is: if wide sections of British society are obsessed with Nazi Germany, why is that the case? We might also ask: is it the case that this is simply a British obsession?

The Nazis and the wider world

In 2000 the American historian Deborah Lipstadt was the subject of a libel action brought by the British writer, David Irving. The action was taken in response to Lipstadt's characterisation of Irving as a 'holocaust denier', that is someone who challenges the truth of accounts of the Nazis' extermination of the Jewish people, and who, in Irving's case certainly denied that Hitler had knowledge of it.[2] In the event Irving lost the case. What, though, was interesting about the case from our perspective was what it revealed about the extent of the debate generated by interpretations of the Holocaust. In January 2000 one newspaper article referred to at least five different critical positions on the history of the Holocaust.[3] The most controversial was that taken by Irving himself, who had denied the existence of gas chambers at Auschwitz, claiming that this was a 'myth' constructed by the Israelis to extract financial reparations from the West German government. Lipstadt has interpreted this argument as both an anti-Semitic attack on the state of Israel, and an attempt to rehabilitate National Socialism, purged of the taint of genocide[4].

The article also referred to the work of two American academics, Peter Novick and Norman Finkelstein. Novick argues that the high profile given to the Holocaust was the product of the efforts of Jewish-American leaders in the 1960s. They promoted the Holocaust, he argues, to limit Jewish assimilation into the wider American population, to deal with anti-Semitism, and to justify American support for Israel. Finkelstein argues that the 'Holocaust industry' developed to provide a historical underpinning to validate the creation and continued existence of Israel. What this single article demonstrated is that there is a wide-ranging international interest in the Holocaust as an aspect of the Nazi experience. Furthermore, it also demonstrated that the context which sustains the arguments around this issue, is the continuing controversy over the policies of the state of Israel.

A similar point about the connection between contemporary contexts and history can be made about the protests that marked the 60th anniversary of the bombing of Dresden, in Germany. In the city itself the neo-Nazi National Democratic Party (NPD) marched, carrying balloons, which proclaimed: 'Allied bombing terror – never forgive, never forget'.[5] In the same year German public prosecutors declined to take action against the NPD for describing the bombing of Dresden as a 'Holocaust'. NPD representatives used this term to draw comparisons with the sufferings of Germans and the destruction of Europe's Jews.[6] In using such terminology the NPD appears to be attempting to lessen the impact of the 'Nazi tag' by claiming that if Hitler's regime committed atrocities, so too did the Allies.[7] This concern with history grew out of a situation in which the far-right hoped to exploit the economic difficulties created by German reunification, and smooth their path to power by 'normalising' the Nazi past.

What the above examples suggest is that, firstly, it is not only the British who have a major ongoing interest in the Nazis and the Second World War; and secondly, that interest in those events exists because they continue to have a contemporary significance. Indeed, the Germans have even coined a word, *Vergangenheitsbewaltigung*, which means coming to terms with the past, and refers to the process of dealing with their Nazi past and its consequences.[8]

Britain and the Nazis

At first sight the average Briton might appear to have less reason to be concerned with the Nazis than would Germans, Israelis or people of Jewish background. But the interest is real. When war broke out, one of the first British responses was to disparage the German identity in comparison to the British. The opening sequences of the 1939 film, *The Lion Has Wings*, for example, contrasts images of the peace-loving English with images of the militaristic, goose-stepping Germans.[9] George Orwell made a similar point in 1941, when he argued that if the British army had used the goose-step people would laugh at them.[10] In both of these examples a positive image of British identity was being affirmed in relation to disparaging images of Germans. Or, to put it another way, British identity became, during the war, bound up with powerful and negative images of Germans.

Major and protracted events like war leave a long-lasting imprint on popular culture. This is clearly the case with the Second World War, which became Britain's 'Finest Hour', and which was constantly relived in popular films in the difficult years of the 1950s. As Lewis Gilbert put it, they acted as 'a kind of ego boost, a nostalgia for the time when Britain was great'.[11] So enduring has this process of mutual identification proved that when German and British football officials met in 2005 to discuss the arrangements for Germany hosting the World Cup, one of the issues they discussed was how to shatter the 'stereotypes of German war-mongers'.[12]

National attitudes are, however, often complex and contain contradictory elements. There is, for example, an enduring belief that, whatever else one might say about the Nazis, they were extremely efficient. Hitler, it is claimed, wiped out unemployment and made Germany strong again.[13] As Sir Nevile Henderson, British ambassador to Germany in the 1930s, put it:

> Within four years the number of unemployed had been reduced to an infinitesimal figure, and by 1939 there was a labour shortage estimated at two million ... To the wheels of Hitler's chariot were, in fact, harnessed the amazing power of organisation, thoroughness and discipline of the German nation.[14]

Linked to this notion of economic efficiency Germany also enhanced its reputation for technical innovation under Hitler's rule. It was this perception that led to the scramble by the victorious allies to secure German scientists, at the end of the Second World War. The United States, alone, secured more than 350. In the post-war era this reputation for efficiency and innovation has continued, in more or less subtle ways, to carry the Nazi taint. This is clearly apparent in Stanley Kubrick's satirical film, *Dr Strangelove* (1963), in which a deranged German-American scientist, a key government adviser, can scarcely prevent his right arm rising in a Nazi salute. After 1945 Germany's economic miracle, at least until the problems caused by reunification, acted as a mirror image of Britain's difficulties and relative decline; it was a process that excited envy and a sneaking admiration. This is reflected in the high status of German products produced by companies like Siemens, Braun and BMW.[15] The Audi company deliberately pitches its products using this apparent technological superiority by incorporating its company motto: *Vorsprung durch Technik* (advantage through technology), in its advertising campaigns.

Past and present

The enduring fascination with the Nazi era has produced a massive number of publications; in 1997 it was calculated that a grand total of 120,000 works had been produced on Hitler alone.[16] This level of interest reflects the enduring legacy of that period. Interpretations of that period are used to justify and attack the policies of governments; underpin national identities, and even shape the language and terminology of contemporary politicians; in 1994, for example, the German Green politician, Daniel Cohn-Bendit, compared the attitude of the United Nations towards the Bosnian Serbs, to the appeasement of the Nazis before the Second World War.[17] The sustained interest in the Nazi era is not, then, simply the product of prurient curiosity, although that does exist, but comes from the enduring relevance of that period and its impact. It is now necessary to turn to the published interpretations of those developments.

Pinning the blame

In the inter-war period British politicians fell into two groups: those who viewed Hitler as a dynamic national leader, and those who found both his methods and objectives totally objectionable. The first group contained most of the Conservative Party, and the second those on the left of the political spectrum. The practical consequence of this division was the policy of Appeasement, which was based on the view that it was possible to satisfy Hitler's 'legitimate' demands, and avoid war. The outbreak of the Second World War dramatically demonstrated the failure of that policy. It also marked the point at which opponents of Appeasement began to develop a particular analysis of Nazism to discomfit its erstwhile supporters. According to this view, Hitler's desire for war and conquest was clearly apparent from the publication of *Mein Kampf* in the 1920s. The political advantage of this interpretation was that it served to demonstrate the folly of attempting to satisfy Hitler. In 1939, Harold Nicolson published *Why Britain is at War* which contained the following passage:

> It seems almost unbelievable that any foreign Government, possessing knowledge of Adolf Hitler's origins and previous record, having before

their eyes the document in which he had confessed the unlimited scope of his ambitions ... could still have hoped that this anarchist could be satisfied by minor concessions or controlled by reasonable persuasion.[18]

The view that the war was a product of Hitler's long-term intentions seemed to strike a chord with the British population. After its first appearance in November 1939, this Penguin Special was re-issued three times, in November 1939, December 1939 and February 1940. This interpretation was powerfully reinforced during the war by the publication of a number of bestselling pamphlets. The first of these, *Guilty Men*, which appeared in the immediate aftermath of the Dunkirk evacuation, linked that defeat to the failure of British politicians to recognise Hitler's clearly stated ambitions.[19] This single work sold 250,000 copies.

The high level of interest in the Hitler period continued after the war. One example of this was the success of William Shirer's *The Rise and Fall of the Third Reich*, which first appeared in 1959. Shirer saw the policies of the Third Reich as the product of Hitler's intentions, for he referred to *Mein Kampf* as a 'blueprint' for genocide against the Jews and foreign conquest.[20] More controversial was Shirer's claim that Nazism developed out of Germany's historical experience. Speaking of the Thirty Years War in the seventeenth century, Shirer declared:

> Germany never recovered from this setback. Acceptance of autocracy, of blind obedience to the petty tyrants who ruled as princes, became ingrained in the German mind.[21]

It is perhaps not surprising that this bestselling work by a journalist should attract considerable academic criticism. It was argued by one German historian that Shirer's work presented the whole of German history as leading towards the establishment of the Nazi regime.[22] Whatever the validity of such criticism, it seems likely that Shirer's book did so well because it satisfied a popular need in the English-speaking world, that of providing an account which explained the war in terms of the intentions and actions of a uniquely evil individual, at the head of a uniquely evil people. This was an account which provided a clear narrative of moral superiority, a feature which no doubt accounts for its enduring popularity. Moreover, one could find very similar views expressed in works from impeccably academic sources. Alan Bullock, in his bestselling biography, *Hitler: a Study in Tyranny*, which first appeared in 1952, also stressed the view that Nazi Germany was, in effect the expression of Hitler's will.[23] Bullock also argued, like Shirer, that Nazism was rooted in German history.[24]

Hitler and post-war Germany

Views such as those expressed by Shirer and Bullock, which stress the centrality of Hitler's intentions, formulated prior to gaining power, to the policies and actions of the Third Reich, have become known since 1981 as 'intentionalist' interpretations.[25] In the English-speaking world 'intentionalism' sought to attribute responsibility for the outbreak and consequences of the Second World War. Alan Bullock makes this absolutely clear in his biography of Hitler.[26] Daniel Goldhagen adopted the same approach in his 1996 book, *Hitler's Willing Executioners*.[27] The 'intentionalist' interpretation stressed the centrality of Hitler's role and the complicity in his actions of a very large section of the German population. In Germany the immediate aftermath of the war saw the publication of a number of works, like Friedrich Meinecke's *The German Catastrophe* (1946), which also stressed the centrality of Hitler's role. However, such works did so to exonerate, as far as they could, the German people. As Ian Kershaw points out, such books sought to pin the responsibility for the war on the demonic figure of Hitler.[28] Furthermore, these writers tended to explain the growth of Nazism as the product of the disturbances that characterised Europe in the inter-war period. This approach, therefore, downplayed the specific responsibility of the German people for what occurred between 1933 and 1945.

It is not difficult to understand this difference of emphasis. Historians like Meinecke and Gerhard Ritter, who had not been Nazis, were aware that historical interpretations of the Nazi period could have an impact on the nature of the Germany that would emerge after the war. They could be seen to be attempting to salvage Germany's cultural heritage from the taint of Nazism.

Conservative and liberal critics of Nazism also had to attempt to circumvent the Marxist view of Nazism, which was that Nazism was the inevitable product of capitalism in the final stages of its decline.[29] What was required was a critique that would denigrate Nazism, but exonerate capitalism. One of the simplest German versions of the attempt to distance the German people from Hitler was also one of the earliest. In 1939, the German industrialist Fritz Thyssen broke with Hitler and fled to Switzerland. In 1941, he published *I Paid Hitler*, an account of his role in the development of events in Germany up to the declaration of war. According to Thyssen's account: 'Hitler deceived me, as he has deceived the German people as a whole and all men of good will.'[30] One might think that, after the Second World War, English speakers would not be susceptible to arguments such as these, even if presented in more sophisticated forms; and indeed we have seen that this is indeed the case. However, external events and the work of political scientists combined to make some aspects of this type of argument quite acceptable.

The Cold War and totalitarianism

Within three years of the end of the Second World War the Cold War began. This was a conflict between, from a western perspective, freedom and democracy, on the one hand, and an oppressive communism on the other. In this context the Marxian analysis of Nazism as the logical outcome of capitalist decline was assiduously promoted in the territories dominated by the Soviet Union, and extremely unwelcome in the western world. It was in this context that the idea of totalitarianism was promoted. It is always necessary to draw a distinction between the motives of academics and the uses made by others of their ideas. Having said this, some ideas flourish far beyond academic life because they make a strong connection with contemporary events. This was the case with 'totalitarianism' in the 1950s. Totalitarian theorists argued that the Soviet Union and Nazi Germany were both regimes of the same type. The political scientist, Carl Friedrich drew up a checklist of six defining features, which applied to both the Soviet Union and Nazi Germany: an official ideology; a single mass party; terrorist police control; monopoly control over the media; a monopoly of arms; and central control of the economy.[31] In the post-Second World War period, the defining features outlined by Friedrich were seen as characteristic of the Soviet Union and the Eastern bloc, but, of course, no longer of Western Germany. Totalitarianism, as a theory, could therefore be seen as simultaneously demonstrating the benefits of free market democracy and placing Soviet-style communism on a par with Nazism.

There was an even wider context to these intellectual developments. Immediately the Second World War ended the Allies seriously considered the possibility of removing Germany's capacity to wage war by permanently destroying her industrial base. However, by the late 1940s the western powers had come to regard the Soviet Union as their most likely future adversary. In that context it was seen as important to build up the economic and military capacity of the newly created Federal Republic (West Germany), rather than destroy it. The decision to build up West Germany's military forces, taken in the mid-1950s, was controversial and provoked protest movements throughout Western Europe. What western leaders required was a device that would allow them to separate the notion of the German military from the Nazi past. A combination of some forms of 'intentionalism' and totalitarian theory enabled this to be effected. Once, therefore, the 'totalitarian' regime powered by Hitler's intentions was destroyed, then, of course Germans could resume their place amongst the other democratic nations. This perspective perhaps explains why Winston Churchill felt moved to tell his constituents, at the height of the controversy over West German rearmament that, in 1945, he had instructed Field Marshall Montgomery to keep surrendered German weapons ready for re-issue to German troops, should they be needed to defend the West against the Soviet Union.[32] The division of Germany's pre-1945 population into 'good Germans', including the German army, and 'evil Nazis' was also strongly represented in popular culture. The 1951 film, *The Desert Fox* for example, counterposed the honourable soldier, Field Marshall Rommel to a fanatical and insanely unreasonable Hitler. Such a depiction was less than totally accurate, but it was one that made the sight of a new German army more palatable to British and American observers.

Those academics, like Karl Dietrich Bracher, author of such works as *The German Dictatorship*, who attempted to apply the concept of totalitarianism to the study of Nazism, found themselves confronted with a number of problems. These were primarily that the models developed by Arendt and Friedrich were static in character, that is, they could not account for the specific characteristics and trajectories of the regimes they were applied to. As one commentator put it:

> In the 1950s, *The Origins of Totalitarianism* engendered much doubt, especially by drawing parallels between Nazi Germany and Stalinist Russia (despite their obvious ideological conflicts and their savage warfare from 1941 to 1945).[33]

According to Ian Kershaw, Bracher responded to these problems by developing his own particular usage of 'totalitarianism'.

> The decisive character of totalitarianism lies for him in the total claim to rule, the leadership principle, the exclusive ideology, and the fiction of identity of rulers and ruled. It represents a basic distinction between an 'open' and a 'closed' understanding of politics.[34]

However valuable this might be as an approach, it does rest on an implicit assumption that the western democracies were and are open societies, and therefore good, and that the societies of the Eastern bloc were not open, and therefore bad. This may seem like common sense to many readers, but developments in the 1960s were to call some of these assumptions into question.

The impact of the 1960s

The early 1960s saw the easing of Cold War tensions, after the Cuban missiles crisis in 1962. This made it easier for critics of the western democracies to give voice to their views. It is worth remembering that the 'witch-hunts' initiated by Senator McCarthy in the early 1950s had largely silenced the expression of left-wing views in the United States. A series of international events, culminating in the Vietnam War, called into question the idea that western powers played an essentially benign role in world affairs. A significant number of, particularly young, people also became increasingly dissatisfied with the materialistic lifestyle engendered by the prosperity of the 1950s and 1960s. Such discontents brought to the fore radical critics of western democracy, like Herbert Marcuse, a German-Jewish exile from Nazism who was an American-based academic by the 1960s. In 1964 Marcuse published *One Dimensional Man*, in which he argued that the media, culture, advertising industry and industrial management in western democracies all worked together to promote a single, uniform view of society and social possibilities.[35] Views such as these tended to blur the distinctions drawn by Bracher between closed and open views of politics; indeed the analysis advanced by Marcuse made the western democracies seem like closed societies, albeit of a different kind.

Developments of this kind stimulated many intellectuals to look more closely and critically at their own societies. In Germany this occurred across the spectrum of academic and artistic activity. In 1970, for example, the German film director, Rainer Werner Fassbinder, declared:

> I would say that in 1945, at the end of the war, the chances which existed for Germany to renew itself were not realized. Instead the old structures and values, on which our state rests, now as a democracy, have basically remained the same.[36]

In other words, for Fassbinder, West Germany rested on the structures and values of the Nazis.[37] Historians also began to subject Germany to a similar close scrutiny.

As a consequence of this process a new interpretation of Nazism emerged, which is variously called 'structuralist' and/or 'functionalist'. The name are used interchangeably, and refer to the concern of historians like Martin Broszat and Hans Mommsen, with the political structures of National Socialism and how they functioned. In their work, as Broszat makes clear, they set themselves against earlier interpretations, such as those of the 'intentionalists', and those who used the concept of totalitarianism.[38] One of the concerns of these historians was with the nature of Hitler's role as leader. 'Intentionalist' writers, as we have seen, present Hitler as the author of *Mein Kampf* and, therefore, the author of the Nazi

Party's programme and ideology. Broszat argues, in opposition to this, that the Nazis had no real ideology. This is not to deny that there were certain fixed points in the Nazi outlook, like an implacable and irrational hatred of the Jewish people, rather it is to deny that these views constituted a fully worked out political philosophy. Instead of this, Broszat argues that Hitler appealed to the Germans on an irrational level as a charismatic leader who embodied their many discontents: 'He voiced what they secretly thought and wanted, reinforced their still unsure longings and prejudices, and thereby created for them a deeply satisfying self-awareness and the feeling of being privy to a new truth and certainty.'[39] In this account, it is argued that, prior to 1933, the ideas of Nazism did not operate as a political programme, but rather as a body of propaganda designed to mobilise the nation to gain power.

This account is, perhaps, rather less palatable to many Germans than some versions of 'intentionalism', because it rejects the notion, as Thyssen puts it, that the Germans were 'deceived' by Hitler, and replaces it with an interpretation that claims he actually articulated the views of the German population. It is also interesting to note that this view of Nazism is very close to some aspects of early Marxist writings on the subject. In 1933, for example, Leon Trotsky wrote, 'Not every exasperated petty bourgeois could have become Hitler, but a particle of Hitler is lodged in every exasperated petty bourgeois'.[40] This is not to say that Broszat was directly influenced by Trotsky, but it does give an indication of the radical implications of Broszat's interpretations, and the radicalism of the time in which they first appeared.

Broszat further argued that the nature of the Nazi movement produced a government of a very distinctive kind. Hitler had no interest in day-to-day routine administrative work, and tended to withdraw from it. However, he also tended to support the creation of autonomous organisations, like the SS, which drew their authority directly from him, rather than central government. This had two consequences: first of all it created a competition for access to Hitler, and secondly, it created a regime in which only he, as the embodiment of the movement and the nation, could resolve internal party conflicts.[41] This presents a picture of the Nazi state as being governed in an erratic and chaotic fashion, depending upon who had Hitler's attention at any particular time. It is a very different picture from that of the machine-like efficiency that is popularly seen as characteristic of Hitler's Germany.

This view also had implications for the Nazis' most notorious action, the attempt to murder the Jewish population of Europe. This was not, according to Broszat, the result of the desire to carry out 'pre-fabricated long-term ideological aims'. Rather it was the product of many interlocking processes, including the accelerated fragmentation of authority into a number of competing organisations.[42] In that situation, it is argued, organisations and individuals sought to enhance their status by over-fulfilling what they interpreted to be the Führer's will. This in turn created the momentum for the deployment of increasing levels of brutality towards the Jewish people, culminating in mass extermination. As Broszat puts it:

> the previous laws and decrees which step by step had further discrimi-
> nated against the Jews in Germany, had subjected them to emergency
> laws and had condemned them to a social ghetto, paved the way for
> the 'final solution'. The progressive undermining of the principle of
> law through measures cast in legal form finally resulted in an utterly
> crude, lawless, criminal action.[43]

A detailed account of this process is contained in the second volume of Ian Kershaw's biography of Hitler. He outlines how, in the period from June 1941 when the Germans launched their attack on the Soviet Union, to March 1943, the Nazis abandoned plans to evacuate the Jews of Europe to the desolate areas of the East, and espoused the full horror of the 'Final Solution'. This process had many different elements. It included the enthusiastic escalation of violence against Soviet Jews by many different elements of the German forces, including the regular army. SS *Einsatzgruppen* (Special Groups), instructed by Hitler to eliminate the 'Bolshe-vist-Jewish intelligentsia', in the early stages of the invasion, used this order as a justification for the mass killing of Jews. In a twenty-day period one *Einsatzkommando* shot 4,400 Jews in Lithuania.[44] A few months later another *Einsatzkommando* claimed to have killed 33,771 Jews in the Ukraine. This appalling escalation in brutality came about to a large degree because Himmler, the head of the SS, who had authority over the conquered territories of the East, was, as Kershaw put it, catching 'Hitler's Mood'.[45]

Despite the mass murder that was ongoing from the moment German forces entered the Soviet Union, Kershaw argues that even the Wannsee conference, called to discuss the 'final solution' of the Jewish problem did not orchestrate 'an existing and finalized programme of mass exterminations or death camps'; instead, the conference initiated a mass deportation of Jews to the East.[46] This was partly in response to America's entry into the war, for which the Jews were held responsible by the Nazis, and partly in response to Stalin's brutal deportation of the Volga Germans to Siberia, for which the 'Jewish-Bolshevists' were also seen as being responsible. The Volga Germans were the descendants of Germans who had settled in Russia in the eighteenth century, and who were regarded by Stalin as untrustworthy. Ultimately, it was the failure to decisively defeat the Red Army that led to the industrial destruction of the Jews in death camps. The unresolved military situation meant that Europe's Jews could not be worked to death or starved in the wastes of Asiatic Russia, and therefore, in Nazi logic, they had to be destroyed by other means. The analysis that Kershaw presents is one in which Hitler's virulent and irrational hatred of the Jewish people interacted with the structures of Nazi government and international developments to create a situation where the regime adopted ever more extreme measures to deal with what they regarded as the 'Jewish problem'; 'structuralist' historians describe this as a process of radicalisation.[47]

'Intentionalism' versus 'structuralism'

It is all too easy when presenting a historical debate to make the positions of the protagonists appear to be rather more polarised than they actually are. Such debates are not really characterised by fixed positions. They are in actuality dynamic interactions within which a multitude of positions may be apparent. Ian Kershaw is Britain's foremost historian of the Nazi period, and it is clear that his work inclines towards the 'structuralist' position. However, there are subtle differences, as he himself has noted, between his interpretation of the Nazi state and that advanced by the German 'structuralist' historians. To take one example, Kershaw points out that Mommsen and Broszat see the development of the Holocaust as coming primarily out of local initiatives, which were given retrospective approval from above. One consequence of this interpretation is that 'Hitler's personal role can only be indirectly induced'.[48] Against this, Kershaw praises the work of an East German historian, Kurt Patzold in the following terms:

> While his description of the process which led from the aim of expulsion to genocide matches the 'structuralist' explanations of western historians, Patzold relates this to a sense of dynamic 'purpose' and direction of the Nazi regime which sometimes appears to be missing from 'structuralist' accounts.[49]

What Kershaw is saying is that while he accepts the account of the process that led to genocide against the Jews put forward by Broszat and Mommsen, he feels that they fail to identify the source of the guiding idea that informed that development. That such is indeed the case becomes evident in the conclusion to the chapter where he states that Hitler's 'intention' was a fundamental factor in the process of radicalisation in anti-Jewish policy which culminated in extermination.[50] In saying this Kershaw does not mean an intention formed by Hitler in the early 1920s to exterminate the Jews. He is arguing, instead, that Hitler's intention to remove the Jews from all German territories, however defined, was the key force driving the Nazis towards the mass murder of the Jewish people. The significance of this for students of historiography is that Kershaw's 'structuralism' is not a simple re-production of Broszat's; but a development from it.

Christopher R. Browning has also suggested modification to the 'structuralist' position. He rejects the 'intentionalist' view that the Holocaust was the fulfilment of a long-term plan formulated by Hitler in the 1920s, but he has argued that Hitler played a much more direct role in the process leading to the Holocaust than has been suggested by Broszat, or even Kershaw. One of the problems confronting historians dealing with this issue is that Hitler's comments on the subject of the Jews, while often violent and offensive in the extreme, were also extremely general in nature, a point that Browning acknowledges.[51] Nevertheless, Browning argues that Himmler, the head of the SS, 'responded to those signals with extraordinary alacrity and sensitivity'. Consequently, he concludes, 'From September 1939 to October 1941 the evidence indicates that Hitler instigated and approved every major change in Nazi Jewish policy'.[52] Browning thus posits a kind of short-term 'intentionalism', and combines it with an acceptance of the structuralists' view of the fragmented nature of German government. His interpretation is also, therefore, like Kershaw's a significant modification of the 'structuralist' interpretation.

In the examples of Browning and Kershaw, the terms of the debate between 'structuralists' and 'intentionalists' have shaped, but not contained the nature of their respective interpretations. This is often the case with historiographical discussions. The wise historian does not aim to produce final answers, but rather to contribute to an ongoing and developing process of investigation and elaboration. One should also recognise that the dominance of a particular interpretive framework does not automatically mean the extinction of other approaches. Michael Burleigh's *The Third Reich: A New History* approaches its subject in a very different fashion. He employs two overlapping models in his study: firstly, he categorises Nazism as a political religion;[53] and secondly, he uses the concept of totalitarianism to link Nazi Germany to the Soviet Union.[54] The two models overlap because, in Burleigh's view Soviet Communism was also a political religion. The concept 'political religion' may well be useful in analysing the irrationalities of Nazism, but there appear to be difficulties in applying the model to Soviet Communism. The Soviet regime, particularly under Stalin, certainly demonstrated many irrational qualities, however, adherents to its doctrines could point to many developments in the world, especially in the inter-war period that seemed to provide empirical evidence for certain key beliefs. Just to take a few: the Wall Street crash and the subsequent depression did, for many, appear to demonstrate that capitalism was in a state of terminal decline and colonial empires did seem to demonstrate the existence of exploitative imperialism. It could, therefore, be argued that Marxism, the official doctrine of the Soviet Union, had a rational basis. National

Socialism, on the other hand could point to very little empirical evidence to support its key political doctrines. Where, for example, could one find concrete evidence that the Jews of Wall Street were in collusion with the 'Jewish-Bolshevists' of Moscow, united in a plot to secure Jewish world domination? Such evidence plainly did not exist, and to believe in such a plot was essentially an act of faith. Burleigh's use of totalitarianism also seems problematic; as we have already noted it is a concept that often ignores differences between the regimes that it links. Indeed Burleigh himself notes a number of key differences between Nazism and Communism.[55]

Normal history

The models which Burleigh employs may well be linked to the purpose of his book, which Richard J. Evans identifies as the desire to write a 'moral history of the Third Reich'.[56] Perhaps it would be more accurate to say that Burleigh wanted to write a moral condemnation of the Third Reich. He makes his approach clear at the beginning of his work:

> This book is about what happened when sections of the German elites and masses of ordinary people chose to abdicate their individual and critical faculties in favour of a politics based on faith, hope, hatred and sentimental collective self-regard for their own race and nation.[57]

The establishment of the Nazi regime in this light can be seen, then, as the product of the moral failure of a large part of the German people. The consequence of this choice was a departure from the norms of western civilisation on a massive scale that has subsequently become a unique and aberrant historical episode.

> There is no 'normal' history somehow adjacent to, or detached from, the fact of the Holocaust, which breaks the bounds of whatever intellectual framework we variously impose upon it.[58]

Here Burleigh has contributed to another continuing debate on the Nazi period: the degree to which it can be seen as a historical development like, for example, the Industrial Revolution, or the War of Spanish Succession.[59] One of the earliest manifestations of this debate appeared in an article by Martin Broszat, published in

1985, when he addressed the problem of what he called 'histori-cization'. What he meant by this term was the process by which the Third Reich could come to be regarded as a historical episode, rather than primarily as a focus for moral condemnation. Broszat further argued that viewing the Nazi period as an exceptional in-terlude had the effect of distorting German history. Kershaw ar-gued that Broszat wanted to apply 'the normal rigours of historical enquiry' to the Third Reich, with the objective of understanding the complexities of the period.[60] Broszat's article provoked a very strong response. The principal criticism of his attempt to 'normalise' the history of the Third Reich was that this would, in the process, 'normalise' genocide, the most significant act of that regime.[61] According to many historians the absolute and unique horror of the Holocaust permanently excludes it from normal history. As Isaac Deutscher put it:

> The fury of Nazism which was bent on the unconditional extermina-tion of every Jewish man, woman and child within its reach, passes the comprehension of a historian, who tries to uncover the motives of human behaviour and to discern the interests behind the motives.[62]

This view raises many important issues for historians because it claims that the Holocaust is literally beyond the abilities of histo-rians to understand. However much one might sympathise with that view, one has to ask certain questions about it. How horrific does an event have to be before it passes human understanding? Can historians, for example, deal with the genocidal massacres in Rwanda in the late twentieth century? The Holocaust was un-doubtedly an absolutely appalling human experience, but to place it beyond historical comprehension seems like an abdication of the necessity to make the attempt to understand it.

There are other German historians calling for the 'normalisation' of the history of the Third Reich who do so from a very different position to that advanced by Broszat. In the mid-1980s West Ger-man historians became engaged in a bitter dispute about the in-terpretation of German history in the Hitler period, which became known as the *Historikerstreit* (historians' dispute). One of the key figures at the heart of this dispute was the well-established histo-rian, Ernst Nolte. In 1986 Nolte published an article in the

Frankfurter Allgemeine Zeitung in which he claimed that the Nazi extermination policy was simply one of many atrocities that characterised the twentieth century; and secondly, that Nazi policies were essentially a defensive response to the threat posed by the Soviet Union, committed as it was to the 'class murder' of its enemies. 'Was not the class murder the logical and factual precedent for the race murder conducted by the National Socialists?'[63] Nolte also argued that Hitler's internment of the Jews was justified because in 1939 Chaim Weizman, a Zionist leader, declared that all Jews would fight against Nazism, even though not all Jews were Zionists, and Weizman had no military forces that he could deploy against the Nazis.[64] In his writings, spread over many years, Nolte has moved from arguing, like Broszat, that Nazi policy had a rationale, to a position of claiming that it was, in some respects, rational, and even, indeed, justifiable. These attempts to 'relativise' the history of the Nazi period, that is to lessen its impact by relating it to what are presented as similar kinds of events are seen by many historians, like Deborah Lipstadt, as an attempt to create a more positive sense of German identity.[65]

The controversial accounts of Nazi actions given by writers such as Nolte and David Irving have brought to the fore in a very dramatic fashion ongoing debates about the very nature of historical enquiry. These debates developed as a consequence of the growing influence of postmodernism in academic life. This development is discussed in Chapter 2, but it would be useful to remind ourselves of some of the positions adopted by those who are covered by this umbrella term. For postmodernists all human experience is contained in language that has no connection with an external reality. Hence, for example, if we say the word 'table' we are simply using a word, not referring to an external object with specific table qualities. To put that another way, we, as the users of the word, put meaning into it, not some inaccessible external reality. If it is impossible to connect with the external world in the present, then it is certainly impossible to connect with it in the past. Consequently, for postmodernists the historians' evidence does not provide access to the past; whatever meaning a historian claims that it has comes, in the postmodernist view from the historian, in the present, who uses it to construct a 'narrative'.

The implication of these views is that historical analyses based on a close scrutiny of the evidence lose all claim to objectivity, and further, that no one historical account is better than another; or as Robert Braun puts it in an article called 'The Holocaust and the problems of representation', 'Thus, past "reality" does not exist; in its place are an endless number of realities tantamount to the various judgements and viewpoints one can find in the present'.[66] To put it very simply the logic of postmodernism is that accounts offered by Holocaust deniers are as valid as any other account of the Nazis and their actions. If nothing else this demonstrates that developments in academic life can, potentially, have an impact in the wider world. In this case, as Richard Evans put it, opening 'the way for Holocaust deniers'. Evans, who was the chief defence witness in the Lipstadt libel trial, also argues that the defeat of David Irving was not simply a rebuff for Holocaust deniers, but was also an important public boost for evidence-based historical investigation.[67]

Conclusion

The continuing controversy in Germany about the interpretation of the history of the Nazi period shows that this is not simply an academic question. Indeed, throughout this chapter we have attempted to demonstrate that historiographical issues are intimately connected with political and social developments. In September 2005, for example, members of the British Muslim community called for the abolition of Jewish Holocaust Memorial Day, established in 2001. This is not the place to discuss the validity of this claim, but it is worth noting that some British Muslims felt that the observation of this memorial lessened the status of the sufferings of their co-religionists: 'The very name Holocaust Memorial Day sounds too exclusive to many young Muslims. It sends out the wrong signal: that the lives of [some] people are to be remembered more than others'.[68] The subtext to this demand was also, probably, a desire to enhance the standing of their community in British society. At the beginning of this chapter we cited a report by the Historical Association which talked about the 'Hitlerisation' of British history syllabuses; hopefully what we have shown, in a relatively brief survey of a subject that has generated a massive literature, is that the impact of the Nazi period is still with us, and still has very real political consequences. It might be argued that it is modern consciousness that has been 'Hitlerised', and that the contents of school syllabuses are simply reflecting that fact.

Further reading

Broszat, M., *The Hitler State* (Pearson Educational, 2001).

Burleigh, M., *The Third Reich: A New History* (Pan Books, 2001).

Childers, T. and J. Caplan (eds), *Reevaluating the Third Reich* (Holmes & Meier, 1993).

Kershaw, I., *The Nazi Dictatorship: Problems and Perspectives of Interpretation* (Edward Arnold, 1993).

Leitz, Christian (ed.), *The Third Reich* (Blackwell, 1999).

Renton, D., *Fascism: Theory and Practice* (Pluto, 1999).

Notes

1 The Historical Association, *History 14–19: Report and Recommendation to the Secretary of State* (Historical Association, 2005), pp. 26–7.

2 D. Lipstadt, *Denying the Holocaust* (Penguin, 1993), p. 181.

3 D. Cesarani, 'History on Trial', *Guardian*, 18 January 2000.

4 Lipstadt, *Denying the Holocaust*, p. 23.

5 'Neo-Nazis upstage Dresden memorial', *Guardian*, 14 February 2005.

6 H. Cleaver, 'German ruling says Dresden was a holocaust', *Daily Telegraph*, 12 April 2005.

7 D. Lipstadt has also detected this attempt to promote the idea of moral equivalences in German academic writings. See Lipstadt, *Denying the Holocaust*, pp. 210–11.

8 R. Brutting, 'History in schools and national identity in reunified Germany', in M. Roberts (ed.), *After the Wall: History Teaching in Europe since 1989* (Korber-Stiftung, Hamburg, 2004), p. 49.

9 *The Lion Has Wings*, directed by M. Powell (London Films, 1939).

10 G. Orwell, *The Lion and the Unicorn* (1941), in S. Orwell and I. Angus (eds), *The Collected Essays, Journalism and Letters of George Orwell: Vol. 2 My Country Right or Left* (Penguin, 1970), p. 81.

11 Quoted in J. Ramsden, 'Refocusing "The People's War": British war films of the 1950s', *Journal of Contemporary History*, 33:1, 1988, p. 59.

12 K. Connolly, 'Taming World Cup wild men', *Daily Telegraph*, 8 May 2005.

13 D. Geary, *Hitler and Nazism* (Routledge, 1993), p. 51.

14 N. Henderson, *Failure of a Mission* (Hodder and Stoughton, 1940), p. 39.

15 J. Ardagh, *Germany and the Germans* (Penguin, 1995), p. 104.

16 Christian Leitz (ed.), *The Third Reich* (Blackwell, 1999), p. 1.

17 Ardagh, *Germany and the Germans*, p. 584.

18 H. Nicolson, *Why Britain is at War* (Penguin, 1939), pp. 43–4.

19 M. Foot, P. Howard and F. Owen, *Guilty Men* (Gollancz, 1940), p. 96.

20 W.L. Shirer, *The Rise and Fall of the Third Reich* (Pan, 1964), p. 148.

21 Ibid., p. 122.

22 R.J. Evans, *The Coming of the Third Reich* (Penguin, 2004), p. xvii.

23 A. Bullock, *Hitler: A Study in Tyranny*. First published 1952 (Penguin, 1962), p. 803.

24 Ibid., p. 805.

25 C. Browning, 'Beyond "Intentionalism" and "Functionalism": A reassessment of Nazi Jewish policy from 1939 to 1941', in T. Childers and J. Caplan (eds), *Re-evaluating the Third Reich* (Holmes and Meier, 1993), p. 211.

26 Bullock, *Hitler: A Study in Tyranny*, p. 13.

27 D. Goldhagen, *Hitler's Willing Executioners* (Little, Brown, 1996).

28 I. Kershaw, *The Nazi Dictatorship: Problems and Perspectives of Interpretation* (Edward Arnold, 1993), p. 6.

29 G. Dimitrov, 'The Fascist offensive and the tasks of the Communist International in the struggle for the unity of the working class against fascism' (1935), in G. Dimitrov, *Against Fascism and War* (Sofia Press, 1979), p. 5.

30 F. Thyssen, *I Paid Hitler* (Hodder and Stoughton, 1941), p. 19.

31 Cited in Kershaw, *The Nazi Dictatorship*, p. 21.

32 J. Ramsden, *Man of the Century: Winston Churchill and his Legend Since 1945* (Harper Collins, 2002), p. 305.

33 S.J. Whitfield, 'Hannah Arendt' (Jewish Virtual Library, A Division of the American-Israeli Cooperative Enterprise, 2005), www.jewishvirtuallibrary/.org/jsource/arendt.html, accessed 13 February 2007.

34 Kershaw, *The Nazi Dictatorship*, pp. 21–2.

35 H. Marcuse, *One Dimensional Man* (Routledge, 2002).

36 Quoted in A. Mombauer, 'West German cinema since 1945', in *European Cinema* (The Open University, 2003), p. 29.

37 *The Marriage of Maria Braun* (1978); *Lola* (1981); *Veronika Voss* (1982).

38 M. Broszat, *The Hitler State* (Pearson Educational, 2001), p. xi, p. 359.

39 Ibid., p. 24.

40 L. Trotsky, 'What is National Socialism', in Trotsky, *The Struggle Against*

Fascism in Germany (Penguin, 1971), p. 406.

41 I. Kershaw, *The Hitler Myth* (Oxford University Press, 1989), p. 262.

42 Broszat, *The Hitler State*, p. 359.

43 Ibid., p. 323.

44 I. Kershaw, *Hitler: 1936–1945 Nemesis* (Penguin, 2000), p. 463.

45 Ibid., p. 469.

46 Ibid., p. 493.

47 C. Browning, 'Beyond "Intentionalism" and "Functionalism": A reassessment of Nazi Jewish policy from 1939 to 1941', in T. Childers and J. Caplan (eds), *Reevaluating the Third Reich* (Holmes & Meier, 1993), p. 211.

48 I. Kershaw, *The Nazi Dictatorship: Problems and Perspectives of Interpretation* (Edward Arnold, 1993) p.86.

49 Ibid.

50 Ibid., p. 107.

51 Browning, 'Beyond "Intentionalism" and "Functionalism"', p. 222.

52 Ibid.

53 M. Burleigh, *The Third Reich: A New History* (Pan Books, 2001), p. 10.

54 Ibid., p.14.

55 Ibid., p.12.

56 Evans, *The Coming of the Third Reich*, p. xviii.

57 Burleigh, *The Third Reich*, p. 1.

58 Ibid., p. 811.

59 D. Renton, *Fascism: Theory and Practice* (Pluto, 1999), pp. 93–9.

60 I. Kershaw, *The Nazi Dictatorship: Problems and Perspectives of Interpretation* (Edward Arnold, 1993), pp. 180–2.

61 Ibid., p. 187.

62 Quoted in Renton, *Fascism: Theory and Practice*, pp. 93–4.

63 Quoted in S. Steinberg, 'Right-wing historian Ernst Nolte receives the Konrad Adenauer Prize for Science', 17 August 2000, www.wsws.org/articles/2000/aug2000/nolt-a17.shtml.

64 Lipstadt, *Denying the Holocaust*, p. 213.

65 Ibid., p. 210.

66 R. Braun, 'The Holocaust and problems of representation', in Keith Jenkins (ed.), *The Postmodern History Reader* (Routledge, 1997), p. 421.

67 M. Kustow, interview with Richard J. Evans, *Red Pepper*, 72, June 2000. Quoted in T. Helms, 'Holocaust Day must be scrapped says Muslim leaders', *Daily Telegraph*, 12 September 2005.

7

Cultural history and Marxism

Introduction

The word 'culture' is not an easy one to define. For many people it
means the practices and products of the high arts, a familiarity
with which can earn the distinction of being 'cultured'. Some historical works do indeed use the term in this way, characterising
culture as 'the intellectual and artistic activities of a society'.[1] Al-
ternatively culture can be defined in a broader, more anthropo-
logical sense, to mean the beliefs and values held by a particular
society or social group. Peter Burke draws a useful distinction between what he calls 'learned culture' and 'popular culture'. The
former refers to an articulated and conscious knowledge of the high
arts, primarily by socially elite groups, and the latter the often
unarticulated, but deeply embedded value systems held by the
majority of society.[2] The only qualification that might be made to
this view is to acknowledge that elite groups also have their own
deeply-held, but often unarticulated value-systems. A semi-facetious
example of this can be found in Nancy Mitford's distinction between U (upper class) and Non-U language.[3]

This chapter will focus on cultural history, as an exploration of
beliefs and values, rather than what might be better described as
the history of culture. Having made the distinction, though, it has
to be acknowledged that beliefs are often embodied in works of art
of whatever kind. In Britain, this approach was pioneered by the
Marxist historians associated with the Communist Party Historians'

Group and their work will form the central focus of this chapter. It will, however, also consider the earlier approaches to cultural history, as influences on the Group, and the development of newer theoretical positions that developed both out of and in opposition to Marxism.

Elite social groups occupied, until relatively recently, a disproportionate share of the historical record. This was, no doubt, partly the product of the class orientation of historians, but it was also because such elite groups' ideas, attitudes and beliefs were much more fully documented than those of other social groups. The study of popular culture, as expressed in customs, songs and festival could and indeed was seen as a corrective to this bias.[4] What, it might be asked, distinguishes such an approach to the history of the lower classes from social history? Hopefully a single example can illustrate the distinction between them. In a work published in 1950, J.H. Plumb described the activities of eighteenth- and nineteenth-century machine breakers as 'pointless' and 'frenzied'.[5] This view was challenged by Eric Hobsbawm, who argued that Plumb's view was, firstly, based on the belief that 'the triumph of mechanisation was inevitable', and secondly that he failed to recognise that the machine-breakers were operating rationally, in their own terms. Hobsbawm described such activities as 'collective bargaining by riot'; by this he meant that, in the circumstances of domestic labour, machine-breaking was the most effective way of conducting an industrial dispute.[6] Both historians were exploring an area of social history, but Hobsbawm, unlike Plumb, attempted to take into account the viewpoint of the machine-breakers, and to that extent his work can be seen as 'cultural'. So, it would seem cultural history can be seen as a form of social history, but not all social history can be seen as cultural in its approach.

Hobsbawm, like many of his generation of Marxist historians, tended to apply this cultural approach to the investigation of the plebeian classes, an approach summed up in the phrase 'history from below'.[7] However, it would be a mistake to believe that all cultural history has this social focus; there are also works which deal with the cultural history of the socially prominent.[8] What works of cultural history have in common is the focus on belief systems, and how such systems influence the behaviour of the groups and individuals that adhere to them.

The impact of literary studies

In England one of the earliest academic engagements with cultural history came from a group of English scholars, in particular F.R. and Q.D. Leavis. This husband and wife team looked back to the seventeenth century as a time when, what they called an 'organic society' existed. By this they meant that in that predominantly agrarian society all social groups, both high and low, shared a common culture.[9] This common culture, however, they argued, was destroyed by the processes of commercial and industrial development. As the mass of the population became engaged in repetitive and soulless labour, so they turned to shallow and debased forms of cultural expression that themselves embodied essentially commercial values. Talking of developments in the early twentieth century, Q.D. Leavis declared:

> The effect of the increasing control by Big Business … is to destroy among the masses a desire to read anything which by the widest stretch could be included in the classification 'literature'.[10]

The importance of such work is that it linked historical developments to cultural change, and it presented culture as the embodiment of a way of life, or a social sensibility. It also promoted a positive view of the culture of the past, and clearly regretted its passing. These attitudes can also be found in the work of historians, like E.P. Thompson, who are particularly associated with a 'culturalist' approach. In 1933 Leavis talked about the village craftsmen of his 'organic society' having:

> a fine code of personal relations with one another and with the master, a dignified notion of their place in the community and an understanding of the necessary part played by their work in the scheme of things.[11]

Thompson, writing in 1963, identified the grievances of working people in the early nineteenth century in very similar terms:

> the rise of a master-class without traditional authority or obligations, the growing distance between master and man; the transparency of

the exploitation at the sources of their new wealth and power, the loss of status and above all of independence for the worker, his reduction to total dependence on the master's instruments of production.[12]

Thompson's generation of Marxist historians, intellectually formed in the 1930s and early 1940s, were, according to Dennis Dworkin, steeped in 'English literary culture'.[13] Thus it seems very likely that Leavis's approach to culture as an expression of social values, and his obvious sympathy and attempt to empathise with the culture of the pre-industrial past, was, at the very least a significant influence upon them.

Perry Anderson, a Marxist scholar who emerged from the 'New Left' of the early 1960s, placed a rather different stress upon the work of the Leavises. He saw them as, in a sense, the product of structural features of Britain's historical development. Anderson argued that because Britain's commercial classes did not assume dominance in their society by decisively defeating the aristocracy, but rather, from the seventeenth century, entered into a series of compromises with them, they failed to develop a distinctive cultural identity. In Anderson's terms, Britain's bourgeoisie failed to develop a sense of totality, that is, an overall vision of the nature of their society and its values.[14] The most significant demonstration of this failure, according to Anderson, was the absence of a national tradition of Sociology in the late nineteenth and early twentieth centuries.[15] The fact that the first attempt to understand, sociologically, the value system of Britain's emerging bourgeoisie was produced by a German, Max Weber, could be seen as supporting Anderson's argument. Weber's thesis was that the culture of Protestantism was peculiarly suited to the pursuit of commercial and industrial gain.[16]

The significance of the Leavises, Anderson argued, was that they attempted, in his terms, a 'totalizing' view of British society and its values through the medium of literary criticism. As Leavis himself put it:

> Literature … mattered. It mattered crucially because it represented a human reality, an autonomy of the human spirit, for which economic determinism and reductive interpretation in terms of the class war left no room.[17]

Literature, as defined by Leavis, then, embodied and preserved humane values in opposition to the forces of materialism, however defined. Anderson's approach to this critique demonstrated an important point: that it was possible to see intellectual culture as developing in a close relationship to economic and social developments; or to put it another way, that such developments could be understood in terms of structural social changes.

The most developed application of this approach, within the literary tradition, comes in Raymond Williams's *Culture and Society 1780–1950*, which first appeared in 1958. Williams defined his work as, 'an account and an interpretation of our responses in thought and feeling to the changes in English society since the late eighteenth century.'[18] Williams's argument – very similar, in some respects to Leavis's – was that the development of industrialisation, beginning at the end of the eighteenth century, had tended to erode communal, humanitarian values and replace them with the values of the market. This process was resisted by a long line of writers who through their writings preserved culture as a sphere that stood out against the economic view of social life and acted as 'a mitigating and rallying alternative'.[19] According to Williams, rapid social change forced some social critics to intently scrutinise their society. In the course of this process they created the idea of culture – which Williams frequently defined as 'a whole way of life'.[20] Or, to put that another way, they developed alternative and humane visions of how a society might be governed; a process that, anticipating Anderson, Williams called 'a total qualitative assessment'.[21] The bulk of his book consists of outlines of the beliefs of a series of writers, beginning with Edmund Burke and ending with George Orwell. Williams does make a convincing case that, collectively, the works of these writers constitute a tradition, although of course the writers have been selected by Williams precisely to demonstrate that. Williams also provides an early example of how it is possible to relate the works of writers of both fiction and non-fiction to the contexts within which they lived, and he is in that sense a major pioneer of cultural history. The conclusion of his work, where he talks about fusing the values of the tradition with the social solidarity of the labour movement to create a common culture is, perhaps, the least successful part of the book. There, his essentially political formulations become extremely vague, bordering at times on the mystical.

> There are ideas, and ways of thinking, with the seeds of life in them, and there are others with the seeds of a general death. Our measure of success in recognising these kinds, and in naming them making possible their common recognition, may be literally the measure of our future.[22]

Williams's desire to create a society based on a humane literary tradition could not be expressed in conventional political terms. It could, though, be related to a clear and explicit political initiative that emerged in the 1930s.

Mobilising history and culture: the Popular Front

By 1935 the leadership of the international Communist movement realised that a new initiative was necessary to combat the advance of fascism. This was the genesis of the Popular Front, the idea that broad anti-fascist alliances should be formed, if possible in all states to protect national democratic institutions. This 'turn' meant putting revolution off the agenda. It was also argued that, in order to protect national institutions, Communist parties should mobilise national histories and cultures.

> Mussolini does his utmost to make capital for himself out of the historic figure of Garibaldi. The French fascists bring to the fore as their heroine Joan of Arc. The American fascists appeal to the tradition of the American War of Independence, the traditions of Washington and Lincoln ....
>
> Communists who suppose that all this has nothing to do with the cause of the working class ... voluntarily hand over to the fascist falsifiers all that is valuable in the historical past of the nation, so that they may dupe the masses.[23]

The logic behind this position was that, if Communist parties were to defend national institutions, then they had to do so, in part, by mobilizing their historical antecedents. In Britain one example of how this was tackled was the publication of a pamphlet called *The March of English History*, in 1936. The cover of the pamphlet featured a variety of historical figures associated with constitutional developments, from Simon de Monfort, the thirteenth-century parliamentary pioneer, to Tom Mann, the trade union campaigner and, in 1936, Communist Party member. What is being presented here is a national tradition, or culture, of accumulating rights, achieved as a consequence of political struggles. Three of the figures featured on the cover are poets; two of them, Shelley and Byron, are featured in *Culture and Society 1780–1950*, an indication of the importance of the Popular Front campaign in the formations of Williams's viewpoint. Williams was a member of the Communist Party of Great Britain in the late 1930s.

The Communist Party's emphasis on the virtues of Britain's historically derived culture in the late 1930s are clearly apparent in this passage:

> THE PEOPLE OF ENGLAND! A great nation, millions of men and women desiring above all to live in freedom, in peace and friendship. Proud of their great achievements … in those men and women, such as Capt. Scott, Mallory, and others, whose endurance, skill and courage conquer nature and space for humanity. A people proud of their instinct for fair play, for the rule of law and justice, who wish to be the veritable pillar of peace and democracy in this modern world.[24]

The choice of Captain Robert Falcon Scott and George Leigh Mallory as examples of British achievement was indicative of how far the Communist Party was prepared to go to develop a nationalist political agenda. Scott died, having failed to lead the first expedition to the South Pole, in the early twentieth century, and Mallory died attempting to scale Everest in 1924.

Out of this political milieu emerged a group of young historians – including Eric Hobsbawm, E.P. Thompson, Rodney Hilton, Christopher Hill, John Saville, Victor Kiernan – who would become particularly prominent in the post-war years. After they formed the Communist Party Historians' Group, in 1946, their tendency to focus on the progressive development of British traditions was further stimulated by new political developments. In 1951 the Communist Party of Great Britain adopted a new programme, *The British Road to Socialism*. This, as its name implies, argued that Socialism could be achieved by distinctively British methods. This change of approach also led to an emphasis on the unifying concept of 'the people', as opposed to divisive concepts like social class. If, as James Klugmann argued, the Popular Front allowed the Marxist revolutionary to repossess 'his or her cultural heritage from the past', then the adoption of a specifically national programme pushed that process even further.[25] The process of re-possession would involve, as Rodney Hilton claimed, grasping 'the political and social consciousness of the various classes'.[26] Or, to put it another way, this meant engaging with popular culture as part of the process of defining the radical tradition of the British people.

A good example of the kind of work undertaken was Christo-pher Hill's extended essay, 'The Norman Yoke', which first ap-peared in 1954. The Norman Yoke was a long-held belief in the quasi-democratic nature of Anglo-Saxon institutions and society; all of which were destroyed, according to some versions of the leg-end, by William I and his invading Normans. Over the centuries, but particularly during the mid-seventeenth century versions of the Norman Yoke were used as the basis for assaults on the notion of private property, the restricted franchise and the rule of kings.[27] In this essay Hill examines how this notion varies in form between classes, and over time, but most importantly how it sustained a long tradition of British radicalism. Referring to the work of late eighteenth and early nineteenth-century radicals, Hill stated, 'If Paine looks back to the Levellers, Spence and Evans look back to Winstanley: and all three look forward to the theories of social-ism.'[28] The Levellers and Winstanley, the leader of the Diggers, were seventeenth-century radicals who used the notion of the Norman Yoke to underpin their political views. This notion was not a fully supported historical interpretation, but rather, Hill sug-gests, an articulation of the common people's sense of grievance as they were progressively driven from the land from the sixteenth century onwards. When they asked who was driving them off the land they could answer – 'the French Bastard and his banditti'.[29] What Hill is arguing here is that political radicalism was sustained over centuries by a notion that was essentially a key element of popular culture, an element which, in turn represented a widely held popular outlook.

The impact of 1956

Until 1956 the Communist Party historians had been loyal party members, and had been allowed to pursue their own interests. The only restriction upon their work was, according to Eric Hobsbawm, a kind of self-denying ordinance that stopped them from looking at twentieth-century history, because it was a contentious area for the international communist movement.[30] In 1956 Nikita Khrushchev, the Soviet premier, made a speech denouncing the crimes of Stalin. Later in the same year the Soviet Union brutally suppressed the uprising of the Hungarian people against their domination. These two events led many western communists to re-evaluate their political allegiances; indeed, within a year or so of 1956 all of the leading British Communist historians, except Eric Hobsbawm, had left the Party. These developments did not simply lead them to re-assess their political loyalties – although all remained Marxists – but had an impact on their work as historians as well.[31] Speaking in 1976 E.P. Thompson described his 1963 work, *The Making of the English Working Class* as:

> in a sense a polemic against abbreviated economistic notations of Marxism, which had become very clearly disclosed in the arguments around, inside and outside of the Communist movement.[32]

The point that Thompson was making related to one of the features of Marxism as a doctrine. Marx had stressed the primacy of the economic base of a society as the key determining feature. On this economic base it was claimed developed all the other features of society – the law, education, politics and culture – as elements of a dependent 'superstructure'. Furthermore, Marx had argued, 'It is not the consciousness of men which determines their existence, but their social existence that determines their consciousness.'[33] This was a controversial idea because it was seen by some critics as making people into beings whose actions were determined, beyond their will, by their material circumstances. Thompson's contention was that the leaders of the Soviet Union had used their supposed knowledge of the nature of material circumstances to manipulate their followers. Those Soviet or Eastern bloc citizens who failed to behave as they should could be branded as suffering from 'false consciousness', or worse, as objective counter-revolutionaries. These practices were satirized by Bertolt Brecht in *The Solution*, a poem that he wrote in the immediate aftermath of the 1953 riots by East German workers.

> After the uprising of the 17th June
> The Secretary of the Writers Union
> Had leaflets distributed in the Stalinallee
> Stating that the people
> Had forfeited the confidence of the government
> And could win it back only
> By redoubled efforts. Would it not be easier
> In that case for the government
> To dissolve the people
> And elect another?[34]

It was in response to these developments that Thompson developed an approach that stressed the idea of agency of, that is, direct human action. This attitude is reflected in the title that he selected for his book, *The Making of the English Working Class*; he argued that the working class was not simply 'made' as the economy developed, but that its members made themselves by defining themselves as in opposition to the employers.[35] The process of self-identification, according to Thompson, takes place entirely within the sphere of popular culture: 'Class consciousness is the way in which these experiences are handled in cultural terms: embodied in traditions, value-systems, ideas and institutional forms.'[35] Thompson did continue to acknowledge the importance of economic factors, but his approach placed a very large stress on culture as the key determinant of social identity and action. This emphasis enabled Thompson to push back the development of the working class to the period 1780–1830 because it invested movements like the Luddites with a new meaning and rationality. Such people, in Thompson's view, were not irrational reactionaries standing out against progress, but were expressing their class opposition to developments that threatened their way of life, in their own terms. This was why he talked about rescuing the plebeians of the period from 'the enormous condescension of posterity'.[37] Thompson was clearly a product of the interaction between politics and history outlined here, but he undoubtedly developed the notion of culture as a mode of identification to a higher degree than his peers.

Thompson's 'culturalist' approach had a great influence on a younger generation of socialist historians that emerged during the 1960s and coalesced around the History Workshop movement, established in 1966.[38] These historians tended to focus on small-scale and often marginalised social groups, like criminals of London's East End, and the inhabitants of one depressed north London street.[39] Such studies tended to emphasise the 'real life experience' of their subjects (oral evidence was frequently used) and within that approach a great deal of attention was given to the belief systems of the group under examination. Paul Thompson's 1983 work, *Living the Fishing*, co-authored with Tony Wailey and Trevor Lummis sought, for example, to explain the then success of Scottish fishermen, compared to English fishermen in the large fishing ports, in terms of differing historically-based cultures. At the heart of the argument was the belief that the tradition of family ownership of vessels, and the use of a 'share' system of earnings, based on the value of the catch, imbued Scottish fishermen with a sense of enterprise that enabled them to prosper.[40] The strong sense of the interaction between community culture and working life is also clearly apparent in the following passage:

> because fishing must depend on co-operative team-work at sea, there is a strong disapproval within the inshore communities of forms of behaviour which generate social friction and division: such as arrogance or anger, domineering or displays of wealth.[41]

In both *The Making of the English Working Class* and *Living the Fishing*, communities express themselves through culturally-determined responses; indeed they do not simply respond, they act in response to value systems that have developed over the generations, either to resist capitalist encroachments or to sustain the prosperity of the community. To put this more simply, in this tradition culture is not simply about what you think, it is also about how you act.

The membership of History Workshop overlapped with that of the Oral History Society, established in the early 1970s. Both movements initially saw their role as the recovery of lost experiences of marginalised social groups. However, over time more and more work was devoted to the study of mind-sets and value systems. A collection of essays, *The Myths We Live By*, published in the History Workshop series and based on the proceedings of the sixth international Oral History conference of 1987, was a good example of this process. This work focused on three ideas, which it presented as crucial areas for historical investigation. Firstly, it was argued that individual and collective memories were not simple records of past events, but shaped and edited accounts. Secondly, that in the process of editing memories, individuals and communities created myths; stories whose content and emphasis underpinned the values of the individual or community. Thirdly, that such myths by shaping perceptions of the world, played a key role in determining how people would act.

> We need as historians to consider myth and memory, not only as special clues to the past, but equally as windows on the making and remaking of individual and collective consciousness, in which both fact and fantasy, past and present each has a part.[42]

Amongst other things this approach means that historians have to positively interpret absences and errors of all sorts as part of that shaping process described by Thompson and Samuel. It also implies that culture, in the sense of value systems is or should be the central focus of historical investigation.

Structure versus agency

There were, however, critics of what was referred to as the 'culturalist' approach to history. Not all of these were academic historians. As a Marxist, Thompson, and many of those inspired by him, believed that their work as historians was not simply an academic pursuit but was part of their political activism.[43] As a consequence the work they produced was seen as having a wider than academic significance and attracted the interest of left-wing theorists from a variety of disciplines. Broadly speaking, though, the critics of Thompson's 'culturalism' tended to stress the importance of political and economic structures as opposed to human agency.

In 1964 Perry Anderson published 'Origins of the Present Crisis'

in *New Left Review*. This was also a work of academic/political en-
gagement as it sought to discuss what an incoming Labour government would have to do to bring about fundamental social change.
In his article Anderson analysed the development of British society
from the seventeenth century onwards. In this he claimed that
because the bourgeoisie had failed to decisively break with the aristocracy, it had failed to develop a distinctive ideology and that, as
a consequence, British political life was impoverished. He also
claimed that because of the early onset of industrialisation, the
working class had failed to develop a socialist outlook. Furthermore, the defeat of Chartism, the growth of imperialism and the
general weakness of British intellectual life meant that when, in
the second half of the nineteenth century socialist parties were
formed, they either failed to take root or were burdened with weak,
composite ideologies. The Labour Party's outlook, according to
Anderson, consisted of a 'mixture of adulterated Marxism, trans-
posed Methodism and inherited liberalism'.[44]

In Anderson's view then, culture clearly flowed from the structure – political and economic – of society, not from the collective
actions of social groups. Furthermore, he discounted the notion of
a tradition of English radicalism. Implicit within Anderson's writings was the notion of an ideal model of social development, devia-
tion from which accounted for the perceived weaknesses of British
society: 'The tragedy of the first proletariat was not, as has so often
been said, that it was immature; it was rather that it was in a
crucial sense *premature*.'[45] Thompson took vigorous issue with Anderson in his 1965 polemical essay, 'Peculiarities of the English', and
generated a debate that was still going strong in the early 1980s.
In 1978 Thompson published 'The Poverty of Theory', which was
principally an attack on the work of the French structuralist Marxist, Louis Althusser, then a major influence on a number of English academics, including Anderson. Althusser drew a clear
distinction between what he called 'ideologies' and science. Ideologies were produced he argued, through a variety of institutions
and activities, including the law, education, politics and culture.
They functioned to (falsely) define the roles of individuals within
capitalist society, hence for example, consumerism appears to offer

freedom of choice, but in reality it creates a society in which individual worth is assessed in terms of prestige possessions. Human beings become slaves to labels, if you like. In Althusser's view science represented the route to true knowledge of the real structures of society, and science was the realm of the theoretician/academic.[46]

Thompson attacked this interpretation of Marxism because it downplayed the importance of self-motivated human action; in Althusser's schema most human beings were trapped in a world of delusional ideology. Furthermore, because it posited the existence of social structures that were somehow beyond human control, it appeared in Thompson's view to render them fixed and unchanging.[47] However, Althusser also claimed that what he called 'Ideological State Apparatuses', were 'relatively autonomous', by which he meant they were capable of expressing ideological identities in a variety of ways.[48] For some, like Stuart Hall, leader of the influential Centre for Contemporary Cultural Studies (CCCS) at the University of Birmingham between 1968 and 1979, Althusser, although flawed in some respects, offered valuable insights for the study of culture. Thompson, Hall argued, went to such lengths to stress the centrality of lived experience as the key source for historical investigation that he came close to claiming that events and developments simply spoke for themselves. Hall argued that experience had to be 'interrogated for its complex interweaving of real and ideological elements'. Further, he argued that if one simply read experience as an unproblematic source of information, history would become a succession of events from which no generalised conclusions could be drawn.[49]

The impact of Althusser's ideas can be seen in the studies published by the CCCS in the 1970s and early 1980s. One of these, *Resistance Through Rituals*, examined the phenomena of youth subcultures, developments which could not be understood in simple terms as expressions of the class conflict. Instead the authors present a more complex picture of youth groups attempting to exercise some autonomy in the construction of distinctive identities, but which nevertheless remain constrained within the boundaries of consumer capitalism. As Dick Hebdige said of the Mods of the first half of the 1960s:

The mod combined previously disparate elements to create himself into a metaphor, the appropriateness of which was apparent only to himself … The magical transformation of commodities had been mysterious and were often invisible to the neutral observer and no amount of stylistic incantation could possibly affect the oppressive economic mode by which they had been produced.[50]

Breaking free from the base

According to Dennis Dworkin, Western Marxism, of which Althusser's work was an example, was attractive to the members of the CCCS because it continued to adhere to the idea that the economic base of society was the ultimate shaping force in society, but it nevertheless 'saw politics, ideology and culture as having their own specificity and logic'.[51] However, by arguing that most people only apprehended the world through ideology and never really appreciated what they saw as the scientific reality, Althusser raised the issue of how meaningful that connection between the economic base and the ideological superstructure actually was. This issue would be the central focus of a new school of, mainly French, thinkers who would become known as the poststructuralists.

A key figure in this grouping was Michel Foucault who was, perhaps, the most historically orientated of them.[52] In 1969 he published *The Archaeology of Knowledge*, which explored both the nature of history and historical knowledge. It is interesting to note that Foucault acknowledged the influence of Althusser, whom he described as a producer of work of theoretical transformation, which 'establishes a science by detaching it from the ideology of its past and by revealing the past as ideological'.[53] Foucault developed this idea by arguing that traditionally historians have aimed at producing 'total' history, that is, an account which is shaped and coherent and constitutes a clear world view.[54] This process, he argued, was essentially an ideological one, designed to demonstrate that only one particular line of development was open to any particular society.[55] Although, Foucault defended his reading of Marx, it is clear that this point, about historically defined lines of human development, could apply to many applications of Marxism. Foucault counterposed to linear interpretations a vision of history that emphasised diversity and discontinuity in human experience. Indeed, the use of the term 'Archaeology' in Foucault's title is indicative of his conception of history. Traditional historians, in his view, approach evidence with a view to give it meaning by re-shaping and editing. Foucault's position is that evidence should be analysed, so to speak, where it is found, and in relation to the original position of other sources, in much the same way that an archaeologist would map the position in which artefacts are located on a dig.[56] Such an approach will necessarily produce discontinuities, but it will also avoid the ideological loading of the traditional historical narrative.

Foucault also had a particular view of the nature of evidence. He argued that traditionally historians attempted 'the reconstitution, on the basis of what the documents say, and sometimes merely hint at, of the past from which they emanate and which has now disappeared'.[57] This approach was based on the view that evidence – usually, but not always – in the form of documents, provided a bridge to a past reality; this view was rejected by Foucault:

> The document, then, is no longer for history an inert material through which it tries to reconstitute what men have done or said, the events of which only the trace remains; history is now trying to define within the documentary material itself unities, totalities, series, relations.[58]

So, for Foucault, evidence did not provide the raw materials for historical investigation, it was history, in its own right. This, taken together with the two other related positions that have been identified – that historians cannot legitimately construct long chronological lines of development; and that historians should study evidence in situ like archaeologists – had radical implications for historians. Collectively these positions meant that all historians could do was to examine evidence to determine the views and beliefs of the past; in effect, therefore within Foucault's vision, all history became cultural history.

Clearly, it was one thing for Foucault and other poststructuralists to develop these kinds of perspectives; it did not, though, follow that historians would automatically take them up. Indeed, it can be argued that there was something of a time-lapse before English-speaking historians began to engage with Foucault. However, towards the end of the twentieth century a number of developments occurred that increased the attractiveness of post-structuralism. As we have seen, some feminist historians began to find the class-based analyses of Marxism inadequate for their purposes. The belief that all human experience was contained within ideologically shaped language, enabled them to argue that female identity was a social construct, not a biological given. The collapse of communism called into question the Marxian idea of history having meaning, purpose and direction; it also called into question the centrality of social class as a motivating force in historical development.[59] It was, no doubt, developments like these that led the journal, *History Workshop*, to drop its subtitle: *A Journal of Socialist and Feminist History*, in the mid-1990s. For these reasons, a number of historians, some of them, like Gareth Stedman-Jones, former Marxists, took what became known because of its emphasis upon language and texts, as the 'linguistic turn', and espoused post-structuralism.

The introduction to Patrick Joyce's *Democratic Subjects* provides a very useful outline of what poststructuralism means for historical practice. (See Chapter 3 for further discussion of Joyce's work.) The book is concerned with the question of identity – both social and individual – in nineteenth-century England. At the very outset Joyce states that his work will be a study of subjectivities. This follows from his rejection of the idea that there is a distinction between representation and the real.[60] This idea is amplified in some polemical comments on E.P. Thompson's *The Making of the English Class*. Joyce notes that Thompson's work identifies the 'productive relations' – broadly speaking, the economy – as the starting point for the development of class-consciousness, expressed in cultural terms. Joyce rejects this linkage, and argues instead that one should begin, not end with, culture. This is because, for him, society is not the product of some external reality, like the economy, it is rather an imaginary construct; by this he does not mean that it is illusory, rather that society and social relations exist entirely within the human construct of language. Within this analysis social relations are the product of the way that human subjects imagine them.

The process of imagining social relations, or identities, is seen as involving the development of narratives – a key term for poststructuralists – these are shaped accounts, which rationalise an individual's, or a society's existence. In the case of one of his subjects, Edwin Waugh, Joyce argues that this narrative was composed of three elements: his concern for education, 'the religious narrative of the soul's journey to God', and the historical narratives that underpinned his politics.[61] In the pursuit of these interests Waugh, in Joyce's view, literally created himself.

Language is, though, as Joyce acknowledges, essentially social in character, and therefore the terms used by figures like Waugh are shared. However, as these terms are the building blocks of 'imagined' societies, they do not relate to external entities and are therefore defined by their relationship to other linguistically expressed ideas and concepts. The meaning of a word derives from its relationship to a multitude of other words. This definitional relationship is what is meant by the term 'discourse', a term much used by poststructuralists. However, meanings do not, according to Joyce, remain fixed. The constant process of subjective identification results, he argues, in the constant making and re-making of meanings. The belief that all human relations are subjectively created in language, when combined with the notion of constant re-definition, produces a perception of constant change within the discourses and narratives that constitute human experience. The term that is used to describe this absence of an organising principle – like the growth of constitutional liberties, in the Whig Interpretation of History – is decentring.

History, then, for Joyce and his co-thinkers, is essentially the study of past subjectivities, through the embodiments of language – texts – that have survived. In that sense all history becomes cultural history because it is concerned with the study of perceptions, values and beliefs; indeed, Joyce locates his work within what he calls 'the new cultural history'.[62] He also rejects the notion that historians can explore some independently existing external reality because: 'the only true foundation is that there is no true foundation, only the making of meaning.'[63]

Conclusion

Cultural History is a vast subject. As a consequence a certain amount of editing and selection has inevitably been necessary for this chapter. No mention has been made, for example, of the French 'Annales' school of historians. This group, who took their name from the title of their journal, *Annales d'histoire economique et sociale*, have, since their emergence in the 1920s, always placed a great deal of emphasis on cultural factors. It has been claimed that Marc Bloch, a founder of the group, 'developed an early psychohistory of myth, mass mentalities and the political use of representation.'[64] Mentalities, in this context, is used to denote belief systems held by individuals and social groups. The 'Annales' school, though, extends over at least four generations of historians, from the 1920s to present day, so it is really a subject for study in its own right; however, it is important to note that this 'school' did have a direct influence on some of the people mentioned in this chapter, like, for example, Eric Hobsbawm.[65]

Historians, as poststructuralist colleagues point out, do have a tendency to trace lines of development. In this chapter the general tendency has been to identify a growing emphasis on a 'cultural' approach to history that has developed through a number of theoretical positions: from a 'culturalist' critique of capitalism to poststructuralism via Marxism. While this narrative is broadly correct it is important to note that works exist that fall outside of this structure. Keith Thomas's *Religion and the Decline of Magic*, which first appeared in 1971, could be seen in this light. Thomas's work explored the progressive eradication of popular magical beliefs by the spread of Protestantism in the early modern period. This was a 'cultural' work written from a non-Marxist perspective. However, as always, there are other qualifications that need to be made. Thomas was an ex-student of Christopher Hill, the Marxist historian of the seventeenth century, and he also served on the editorial board of *Past and Present*, a journal that had been co-founded by members of the Communist Party Historians' Group. So, clearly Thomas would have been familiar with the writings of British Marxist historians. Perhaps, what this suggests is that the distinctions between historians are rarely defined in black and white terms, but in a infinite number of shades of grey.

A similar point can be made about poststructuralism. It is undoubtedly the case that some of the historians who have taken the 'linguistic turn' believe that nothing less than the wholehearted espousal of poststructuralism will do. It is equally undoubtedly the case that many working historians do not take that position; however, rather than offering outright opposition most of them are prepared to accept that their work can be enhanced by incorporating cultural concerns into their existing practice. As Miri Rubin puts it:

> For while shame-faced political, hard-nosed demographic, forbidding diplomatic, and chapped-skinned imperial historians were left out of all the good historical party-lists in the 1970s and 1980s, they are now back on them, invited as experts on political rituals, Cold War culture, cultural encounters. The same can be said of the histories of medicine, science and law – spheres which were marginal to the first wave of the 'new' history in the 1960s and 1970s – but have been remade as exciting new areas by those able to probe their 'cultural' making.[66]

Cultural approaches to history have added many new elements to historical investigation, including a much greater stress on questions of identity, and this has undoubtedly increased understanding of the experiences of the past,[67] the crucial point being that such approaches are additions to the existing repertoire of the historian. Those who argued that cultural history, in the form of poststructuralism, is a radical break risk making the same mistake as those who made similar claims for social history and oral history.

Further reading

Dworkin, D., *Cultural Marxism in Postwar Britain* (Duke University Press, 1997).

Evans, R.J., *In Defence of History* (Granta Books, 2001).

Foucault, Michel, *The Archaeology of Knowledge* (Routledge, 2002).

Joyce, P., *Democratic Subjects: The Self and the Social in Nineteenth Century England* (Cambridge University Press, 1994).

Rubin, M., 'What is Cultural History Now?', in D. Cannadine (ed.), *What Is History Now?* (Palgrave, 2002).

Thompson, E.P., *The Making of the English Working Class* (Penguin, 1991).
Williams, Raymond, *Culture and Society* (Hogarth Press, 1987).

Notes

1 C. Harvie, G. Martin and A. Scharf (eds), *Industrialisation and Culture 1830–1914* (Macmillan, 1970), p. 12.
2 P. Burke, 'The "Discovery" of popular culture', in R. Samuel (ed.), *People's History and Socialist Theory* (Routledge & Kegan Paul, 1981), p. 216.
3 M.S. Lovell, *The Mitford Girls* (Abacus, 2002), pp. 452–3.
4 A.L. Lloyd, *Folk Song in England* (Paladin, 1975), p. 22.
5 J.H. Plumb, *England in the Eighteenth Century* (Penguin, 1950), p. 150.
6 E.J. Hobsbawm, 'The Machine Breakers', in Hobsbawm, *Labouring Men* (Weidenfeld and Nicolson, 1968), pp. 5–7.
7 D. Dworkin, *Cultural Marxism in Postwar Britain* (Duke University Press, 1997), p. 79.
8 M.J. Wiener, *English Culture and the Decline of the Industrial Spirit 1850–1980* (Penguin, 1985).
9 A. Samson, *F.R. Leavis* (Harvester Wheatsheaf, 1992), pp. 37–8.
10 Q.D. Leavis, *Fiction and the Reading Public* (Chatto and Windus, 1932), p. 17.
11 F.R. Leavis and D. Thompson, *Culture and Environment* (1933), quoted in F. Mulhern, *The Moment of Scrutiny* (Verso, 1981), p. 50.
12 E.P. Thompson, *The Making of the English Working Class* (Penguin, 1968), p. 221.
13 Dworkin, *Cultural Marxism in Postwar Britain*, p. 43.
14 P. Anderson, 'Components of the National Culture', in Alexander Cockburn and Robin Blackburn, *Student Power* (Penguin, 1969), p. 226.
15 Ibid., p. 219.
16 Max Weber, *The Protestant Ethic and the Spirit of Capitalism* (Unwin, 1930), p. 153.
17 Quoted in Anderson, 'Components of the National Culture', p. 273.
18 R. Williams, *Culture and Society 1780–1950* (Penguin, 1963), p. 11.
19 Ibid., p. 17.
20 Ibid., p. 47.
21 Ibid., p. 285.
22 Ibid., p. 323.
23 G. Dimitrov, 'The Fascist offensive and the tasks of the Communist International in the struggle for the unity of the working class against Fascism', 2 August 1935, in G. Dimitrov, *Against Fascism and War* (Sofia Press, 1979), p. 74.

24 *The March of English History* (The Communist Party of Great Britain, 1936) p. 3.

25 J. Klugmann, 'Introduction: Crisis in the thirties: A view from the Left', in J. Clark, M. Heinemann, D. Margolies and C. Snee (eds), *Culture and Crisis in Britain in the 30s* (Lawrence and Wishart, 1979), p. 25.

26 Quoted in B. Schwarz, '"The people" in history: The Communist Party Historians' Group', in R. Johnson, G. McLennan, B. Schwarz and D. Sutton (eds), *Making Histories* (University of Minnesota, 1982), p. 60.

27 C. Hill, 'The Norman Yoke', in C. Hill, *Puritanism and Revolution* (Penguin, 1990), pp. 92–3.

28 Ibid., p. 111.

29 Ibid., p. 125.

30 E. Hobsbawm, *Interesting Times* (Abacus, 2003), p. 291.

31 Interview with Eric Hobsbawm in H. Abelove et al. (eds), *Visions of History* (Manchester University Press, 1983), p. 33.

32 Interview with E.P. Thompson, ibid., p. 7.

33 K. Marx, Preface to *A Contribution to the Critique of Political Economy* (1859), in Lawrence H. Simon (ed.), *Karl Marx Selected Writings* (Hackett Publishing Inc., 1994), p. 211.

34 J. Willett and R. Manheim (eds), *Bertolt Brecht Poems, Part III 1938–56* (Eyre Methuen, 1976), p. 440.

35 E.P. Thompson, *The Making of the English Working Class* (Penguin, 1968), p. 9.

36 Ibid., p. 10.

37 Ibid., p. 13.

38 R. Samuel, 'History Workshop 1966–80', in Samuel (ed.), *People's History and Socialist Theory* (Routledge & Kegan Paul, 1981), p. 414.

39 J. White, *Campbell Bunk: The Worst Street in London Between the Wars* (Pimlico, 2003); R. Samuel, *East End Underworld: Chapters In the Life of Arthur Harding* (Routledge & Kegan Paul, 1981).

40 P. Thompson, T. Lummis and T. Wailey, *Living the Fishing* (Routledge, Kegan & Paul, 1983), pp. 6, 46.

41 Ibid., p. 166.

42 R. Samuel and P. Thompson, *The Myths We Live By* (Routledge, 1990), p. 21. See also P. Thompson and M. Chamberlain, *Narrative and Genre* (Routledge, 1998), p. xiii.

43 R. Samuel, 'Afterword', in Samuel (ed.), *People's History and Socialist Theory*, p. 415.

44 P. Anderson, 'Origins of the Present Crisis', *New Left Review*, 23, January–February 1964, accessed 13 February 2007 at www.newleftreview.org/

Issue122.asp?Article=03, p.15.

45 Ibid., p. 6.

46 L. Althusser, *For Marx* (New Left Books, 1977), pp. 11–12.

47 E.P. Thompson, 'The Poverty of Theory', in *The Poverty of Theory and Other Essays* (Merlin, 1978), p. 290.

48 L. Althusser, 'Ideology and Ideological State Apparatuses (notes towards an investigation)', in Louis Althusser, *Lenin and Philosophy and Other Essays* (Monthly Review Press, 1971), p. 149.

49 S. Hall, 'In Defence of Theory', in Samuel (ed.), *People's History and Socialist Theory* (Routledge & Kegan Paul, 1981), p. 383.

50 D. Hebdige, 'The Meaning of Mod', in Stuart Hall and T. Jefferson (eds), *Resistance through Rituals: Youth Subcultures in post-war Britain* (Hutchinson, 1976), p. 94.

51 Dworkin, *Cultural Marxism in Postwar Britain*, p. 142.

52 M. Foucault, *The Birth of the Clinic* (Tavistock, 1973); M. Foucault, *Discipline and Punish* (Allen Lane, 1977); M. Foucault, *Madness and Civilisation: A History of Insanity in the Age of Reason* (Routledge, 2001); M. Foucault, *The History of Sexuality* (Penguin, 1990).

53 Michel Foucault, *The Archaeology of Knowledge*. First published 1969 (Routledge, 2002), p. 5.

54 Ibid., p. 11.

55 Ibid., p. 13.

56 Ibid., p. 8.

57 Ibid., p. 7.

58 Ibid.

59 R.J. Evans, 'Prologue: *What is History?* – Now', in D. Cannadine (ed.), *What is History Now?* (Palgrave, 2002), p. 6.

60 P. Joyce, *Democratic Subjects: The Self and the Social in Nineteenth Century England* (Cambridge University Press, 1994), p. 2.

61 Ibid., p. 82.

62 Ibid., p. 3.

63 Ibid., p. 13.

64 M. Middell, 'The Annales', in S. Berger, H. Feldner and K. Passmore (eds), *Writing History: Theory and Practice* (Arnold, 2003), p. 107.

65 Hobsbawm, *Interesting Times*, p. 289.

66 M. Rubin, 'What is Cultural History now?', in Cannadine (ed.), *What Is History Now?*, p. 80.

67 A. Brown (ed.), *Historical Perspectives on Social Identities* (Cambridge Scholars Press, 2006).

8

Conclusion

We have tried to show ways in which a critical intelligence can be brought to bear upon historiography. For the undergraduate readers especially, we have tried to indicate the need for an informed reading of texts. In the rush to complete assessed work there is too often a tendency to strip-mine texts for 'facts' rather than to engage critically with their authors. We have tried to indicate some of the issues to bear in mind when assessing historiographical debates and the extent to which some interpretations depend on wider narratives or preconceived ideas. Our conclusions have tried to avoid simplistic notions of what is right or wrong; we do not provide a template for the historical method. So where does this leave the question of objectivity?

How often do we read that somebody has written 'the definitive' work on some topic? Perhaps not as often as we used to, but unwarily enthusiastic reviewers still make such claims. But the author is no longer always an absent figure, an objective judge. In the nineteenth century, when history was established as an academic profession, the notion of objectivity was often described as a matter of 'science'. Such was the prestige of the natural sciences that 'science' was regarded as an objective ideal to which all branches of learning aspired. This led to unfortunate confusions about whether or not history was a positivist science;[1] and to the debate, now usually regarded as rather pointless, but actually quite educational, between those who supported J.B. Bury's view that history was a science 'no less and no more' and G.M. Trevelyan's defence of history as an 'art' with broad educational values and no especial connection with notions of scientific truth.[2] The legacy of these arguments was not a belief in Positivism, a heretical notion according to most British historians, but a determination to write monographs in such a way that the author's views were supposedly excluded. This had led to several stylistic habits which are embedded in the culture of academia and in publishers' advisory notes. For example, historians have not traditionally used the first person singular, except rarely in prefaces or the occasional footnote, and this can lead to some strange circumlocutions and odd sentence structures.

At the turn of the nineteenth century, this belief in objectivity supposedly peaked with Lord Acton's famous statement (1898) to the contributors to the multi-volume, multi-authored *Cambridge Modern History*:

> Our scheme requires that nothing shall reveal the country, the religion, or the party to which the writers belong. It is essential not only on the ground that impartiality is the character of legitimate history, but because the work is carried on by men acting together for no other object than the increase of accurate knowledge.[3]

However, this did not mean that Acton necessarily expected no exercise of judgement, for on other occasions he had criticised historians who failed to condemn the wicked; he believed, as he had earlier put it, in 'the inflexible integrity of the moral code' which helped to provide the purpose of historical study but today would be met with scepticism.[4]

Since then it would seem that historians have been in further retreat from any claims to truth or objectivity. Two main arguments were used in the mid-twentieth century to defend the objectivity of history. The association of history with social science methods peaked with the adoption of new, supposedly rigorous quantitative techniques; this reintroduced the possibility of scientific objectivity, despite the cliché about lies, damn lies and statistics. The great authority on this approach was Fogel. Criticism of both his general approach and his specific methods somewhat tarnished the initial lustre of this supposed new gold standard. And fewer social scientists came to claim that sort of positivist objectivity.

The other defence was an appeal to history's professionalism: the great exponent of this defence was Geoffrey Elton. The two men, so opposed in terms of their attitude to methodology, especially on the relationship between history and social science, were to combine in defence of objective standards.[5] More recently of course it is postmodernism that has challenged the objectivity, indeed in its most extreme form the very possibility, of history. One of the most combative objections to this influence is Richard J. Evans's *In Defence of History* (1997). Evans picks up many themes, but above all he tackles postmodernism as a danger to scholarship with a serious purpose.[6] In practice, most historians, while recognising the rich variety of historical scholarship and observing the way in which their own profession has always reflected the prevailing culture of its own times, remain convinced that their work has a real relationship to events in the past and that interpreting it according to the evidence as well as according to their own lights, has a very real significance for the future.

It is essential for the health of the subject that historians stick to an assumption that history is evidence-based, and in that sense at least like the natural sciences; and that the task of the historian is to seek an explanation, as well as an account, of how things happen. To do this they do not, and must not, retreat to a bunker and deny the rich variety of historiographical approaches that even a cursory look at the history and the achievements of their own subject can illustrate. They must see the variety and the ever-changing nature of historiography as a strength, not a weakness. The choice of topic and method will be determined by the present context in which the historian works, and this ensures the relevance of history and keeps it dynamic. Equally, historians should not resign from their task of interpreting the history of human actions. If they do not do this, others will and without the scholarly ambition to treat the evidence with honesty.[7]

Of course history is about the past, but historiography is always responsive to present interest and needs. It is a human artefact, so inevitably it is a part of the intellectual life of the society that produces it. Ever-changing, it is always open to criticism and amendment, a characteristic it also shares with science. In its vitality it makes a crucial contribution to a healthy life of the intellect and thus to the health of society.

Just as the history student has to become acquainted with the use and interpretation of primary sources, the essential building blocks of original historiography, so the secondary sources also need to be approached with the understanding that they too are not simply a quarry of received and unchallenged opinion. Their authors have shaped and dressed the material for their own purposes. But, once this is understood, they become invaluable to our own understanding of society. The people who manage higher education sometimes favour vocational study because they can point to its utility and its supposed popularity amongst ambitious students. But the market for vocationally-trained students fluctuates, as does the popularity of particular vocations. Fortunately, employers recognise the skills of selection and discrimination, the understanding and the powers of expression that go with being a good history graduate; and, crucially, the understanding that comes with historical knowledge makes a vital contribution to the democratic health of a nation.

Notes

1   C. Parker, *The English Historical Tradition Since 1850* (John Donald, 1990), pp. 20–40; C. Parker, 'English historians and the opposition to Positivism', *History and Theory*, xxii (1983), pp. 120–45.

2   J.B. Bury, *Selected Essays* (Cambridge University Press, 1930); D.S. Goldstein, 'J.B. Bury's philosophy of history: a reappraisal', *American Historical Review*, 82 (1977), pp. 896–919; G.M Trevelyan, *Clio, A Muse* (Longman, 1949).

3   J.E.E. Dalberg-Acton, *Lectures on Modern History* (Macmillan, 1930), pp. 316, 318.

4   Parker, *The English Historical Tradition since 1850*, pp. 57, 95–6.

5   R.W. Fogel and G.R. Elton, *Which Road to the Past?* (Yale University Press, 1983).

6   R.J. Evans, *In Defence of History* (Granta Books, 1977).

7   We note with pleasure that other texts have been coming to the same conclusions. See, for example, P. Lambert and P. Schofield, *Making Histories: An Introduction to the History and Practices of a Discipline* (Routledge, 2004), pp. 290–7.

Index

Note: 'n.' after a page reference indicates the number of a note on that page.